AUTHORITY
NOT MAJORITY

AUTHORITY
not
MAJORITY

The Life and Times of

FRIEDRICH JULIUS STAHL

Ruben Alvarado

WordBridge
PUBLISHING
Aalten ✦ the Netherlands

www.wordbridge.net

Table of Contents

Preface

This biography fills a void that has existed for far too long in the English language. Friedrich Julius Stahl was one of the greatest statesmen of 19th century Germany. One would not know that, of course, because today he is totally forgotten – even by most Germans. But in the 19th century Stahl played a crucial role in the modernization of Prussia. He also stood as one of the last in a long line of confessing Christian statesmen drawing upon the fast-disappearing common-law tradition of the vanished Holy Roman Empire. His work continued that of Edmund Burke and Friedrich Carl von Savigny, putting conservatism on a solid philosophical foundation. But since he was a Jewish convert to Christianity, and since Christian politics went into eclipse with his death and the deaths of those who shared his vision, Germans concerned to put this period of history behind them felt the need to banish his memory.

In the words of one of Stahl's leading modern biographers, Wilhelm Füßl, "the judgement of the future Reich Chancellor Otto von Bismarck is symptomatic…. At the Erfurt Union Parliament of 1850 he spoke of the 'beloved Stahl,' a few years later he saw him disparagingly only as the baptized Jew…. During the time of Nazi rule the converted Jew Stahl and his conservative thought were completely eliminated from German constitutional law teaching – a further ground for Stahl's virtual oblivion today."[1]

The account given by Peter Drucker, one of the 20th century's leading authorities in management science, sheds

---

[1]"Friedrich Julius Stahl," in Heidenreich, *Politische Theorien des 19. Jahrhunderts: I. Konservatismus*, 188.

further light on Stahl's treatment.[2] One of the few 20th century writers to recognize Stahl's importance, Drucker wrote a short work about Stahl intended, in his words, to "make it impossible for the Nazis to have anything to do with me, and equally impossible for me to have anything to do with them.... A monograph on Stahl, which in the name of conservatism and patriotism put him forth as the exemplar and preceptor for the turbulence of the 1930s, represented a frontal attack on Nazism." The book, published in 1933, was "immediately banned and publicly burned." The publisher, Oskar Siebeck, took his own life in 1936 after fruitless negotiation with the Nazi chamber of literature regarding his publishing agenda. And so Stahl's memory lies buried to this day.

It cannot be helped that this book is of a fragmentary, truncated nature: not much is known of Stahl's private life. Indications of it are to be gleaned from private correspondence, both his and that of other important actors of his time, but the research to uncover those fragments is itself sketchy.[3] Furthermore, this book is intended not to be an exhaustive effort summarizing all available information on Stahl, but rather as an introduction to his life and work to accompany the translation, by the author, of his magnum opus, the *Philosophy of Law*.

As it stands, therefore, this book runs the risk of falling between two chairs. For the layman, its subject matter – legal philosophy, constitutional law – can be rather abstruse. For the one versed in such material, however, the book is much too summary a treatment thereof. If one keeps in mind its purpose, this should not pose an insurmountable problem. For those

---

[2]Drucker's account is conveniently accessible on the Internet at http://www.peterdrucker.at/en/texts/stahl_01.html

[3]For further details, see the bibliography.

interested, the subject matter of law and legal philosophy will be treated in more detail in the *Philosophy of Law*.

This has made the book both difficult and easy to write. Difficult, because of the inherent problem of summing up the work of someone whose writings were both voluminous and deep, and who added to his academic work the career of one of Germany's most accomplished parliamentarians. Easy, because there is virtually nothing in English to which it may be compared or against which it may be contrasted. Even given the shortcomings of the present work, it is far better to have it than nothing at all.

1. Setting the Stage

The Europe into which Friedrich Julius Stahl was born was being transformed by the French Revolution, "the most astonishing that has hitherto happened in the world."[4] Indeed, that Revolution brought cataclysmic changes in its train. The feudal system was swept away along with the monarchy that had rested upon it. France was now ruled by "citizens," *citoyens*, men who had overthrown and executed a king and queen, eliminated an aristocracy, abolished a legal system, and established a "republic" in accordance with the principles of their *Declaration of the Rights of Man and Citizen*. To all appearances, Rousseau's "General Will," the "will of the people," had triumphed over the will of crowned heads.

And it was not only France that was feeling the effects of the "General Will." Across the board, Europe was being fundamentally transformed. For the *citoyens* were on the march, to rid Europe of the same institutions they had successfully disposed of at home. And their efforts met with ringing success: by the time Stahl was born in 1802, continental Europe lay prostrate before the men of the *Marseillaise* and their citizen leader, Napoleon.

What did the Revolution signify? Among other things, it was supposed to establish the famed liberty, equality, and fraternity, through equal rights, representative institutions, and the abolition of antiquated privilege. In practice what it meant was the replacement of burdensome feudal levies by equally burdensome taxation and the rule of an all-powerful bureaucracy. "Military power and bureaucratic control, not political

---

[4]Burke, *Reflections*, 95.

participation and civil liberties, were the true hallmarks of the regime."[5] The keynote was centralization, entailing the destruction of local government and customary law in favor of national legal codes and administration.

Thanks to the triumph of French arms this was accomplished not only in France but across Europe. In order to implement this demolition work, Napoleon realized what no French king had ever done before him, though not for lack for trying. That was to destroy the Holy Roman Empire of the German Nation. The Holy Roman Empire for centuries had functioned as the constitution of Germany; it had served to restrain the more powerful states, like Prussia and Bavaria, from swallowing up the smaller states around them. The Empire was a patchwork quilt of autonomous states, principalities, free cities, even minuscule free knightly estates, legally beholden to none but the Emperor himself. Throughout its history, but especially during the period after the signing of the Peace of Westphalia in 1648, these smaller states had striven mightily to maintain their separate existences. And the constitutional framework of all these states large and small was indelibly bound up in the overall framework of the Holy Roman Empire. It was the Empire, ephemeral though its powers of execution may have been, that provided the room within which all those separate polities could maintain their independence. Rights and liberties, privileges, memberships in the various bodies of estates, all were tied to the Empire. When Emperor Francis resigned the Imperial majesty in 1806, declaring the Empire dissolved, that entire constitutional fabric disappeared with him. Now many of the small states were amalgam-

---

[5]Sheehan, *German History 1770-1866*, 261. Sheehan's remark characterizes Napoleon's makeshift "Kingdom of Westphalia," but it can be generalized.

ated, granted as gifts of conquest to Napoleon's clients. These together formed his buffer state, the Rhine Confederation.

This is what is crucial to understand about the Revolution: it was the continuation of French government policy, both foreign and domestic, by other means. For centuries, the house of Bourbon and before it the Valois had battled with the house of Habsburg, the elected occupant (almost without interruption) of the imperial throne, over control of Germany. At the same time, it had successfully pursued a policy of coopting all areas of independent power in France: the throne increasingly became a spider at the center of an all-embracing web of influence. These tandem efforts had one aim, to realize in ever-heightened degree the omnipotence of the crown – which means, of course, the omnipotence of central government – in two directions, outward and inward, foreign and domestic.

France and the Holy Roman Empire represented two different orders, two different possibilities for Western civilization. The Empire was the continuation of medieval Christian civilization. At its pinnacle stood the two heads of Christendom, the Emperor and the Pope, both sworn to uphold and defend the Christian faith. Its framework was hierarchical yet decentralized, with the feudal framework having evolved into a plethora of semi-autonomous units of government; this framework had developed in terms of historical growth, of the continuous accretion of rights, liberties, and privileges, often confused and contradictory but nevertheless cherished and surprisingly effective in guarding the claims of the weak against the strong. Within the established framework of faith and law, there was considerable freedom of movement. By extension, sovereignty itself was limited. The nations of Europe constituted a community, a shared existence.[6]

France, on the other hand, represented isolation, autonomy, uniformity. "The King of France... saw around him, not [the emperor] Charles's *corpus christianum*, but *Europe*, that is a number of states large and small, a multitude of greater or lesser 'powers', each in its own view sovereign and almost independent, with no more than its own interests to guide it."[7] France pioneered the world of reason of state, of *Realpolitik*, where interests are paramount rather than justice. The community of Christian nations receded in favor of a conception of states and nations merely as competing loci of power.

The conflict between these two orders first came into view in the struggle between the Habsburg emperor Charles V and the Valois king Francis I in the 16th century. "Charles... understood the policy of his opponent perfectly. He did not, however, see that what was gaining ground in contemporary France was a political 'solution', fundamentally opposed to and competing with his own policy; even less did he see that this was an idea which one day would carry the field. He saw in Francis the captain of a ship that had lost its bearings."[8]

The conflict between the Empire and France was obscured by the struggle between Catholic and Protestant. In a sense, this latter struggle ensured the triumph of the "French way." For it was division in the church, and the conflict between countries that otherwise shared the fundamental

---

[6]The Reformation, of course, complicated this situation, but it did not break with it. Although Protestants did not recognize the Pope as head of the church, they did recognize the Emperor as head of the Empire. In fact, the Reformation enabled the German constitution to survive, for it stymied the drive toward centralization. For further discussion on this point, consult Alvarado, *A Common Law*.

[7]Meyer, *Leibniz and the Seventeenth-Century Revolution*, 15.

[8]Meyer, *Leibniz*, p. 15.

world-view of a Christian community of nations, that enabled this new approach to religion, law, and politics, to gain ground.[9] This came about not only militarily, through the destruction of Germany in the wars of religion; it also came about in the realm of the spirit, where the philosophy of humanistic autonomy took hold as an alternative to the continual strife between confessions.

France embodied this new philosophy of human autonomy, of the centrality of the individual will. Louis XIV (1638-1715) self-consciously put this philosophy into practice.[10]

> The most characteristic trait of the age following upon the Thirty Years' War was its attempt to overcome all conflicts by an exertion of the will.... This... was an age in which values came to be designated in terms of the Self, and in which the will became the sole criterion of all activity.... In domestic as well as in foreign politics a new relationship was postulated between the individual and the state, and between the states themselves. France was the first country to realize and to put into practice this new relationship; and thus she became the leading country on the Continent.... The political constitutions of the past, the social order of the feudal Estates with the *respublica christiana* as its highest political principle, stood from now on in direct opposition to the new rationalist constructions of the age.... Three properties characterize the new state. First, the centralization of all powers in one place – Versailles – and in the hands of one person – Louis XIV; secondly, the unification of law, economics and fiscal policy – in Colbert's mercantilism; lastly, the fusion of state and science – in the *Académie des Sciences*, and of state and Church – in the Gallican Articles.[11]

---

[9]See Alvarado, *A Common Law*, pp. 67ff.

[10]These remarks about the significance of France and the crucial importance of this period of European history owe much to Meyer's brilliant exposition.

[11]Meyer, *Leibniz*, pp. 16, 17, 22, 24.

The struggle against the France of Louis XIV was therefore more than a mere attempt to maintain the balance of power in Europe, to keep France from gaining hegemony; it was likewise a struggle to keep at bay a world-view, the implications of which were becoming increasingly clear.

If more people, and especially people in power, had shared Leibniz's insight[12] – envisioning Europe as standing at a crossroads, having to choose between alternative civilizations – then history might have turned out differently. Leibniz realized that the empire needed to be reformed, that the various states needed to be better integrated the one with the other; many of the smaller states shared his viewpoint. He also realized that this conflict was of a piece with the conflict between Christian faith and humanistic autonomy. He understood that the way forward was *not* to jettison this fabric in favor of autonomous statehood, just as little as the church should be jettisoned in favor of societies of knowledge. But the bigger players, such as Austria, Prussia, and Bavaria, had no use for such constraints on their power or freedom of movement. And in this they were only following the other members of the alliance against France: England and the Netherlands, and especially England.

These developments came to a head in the War of the Spanish Succession (1701-1714). Although thoroughly covered by specialists, this war and its significance are virtually unknown to the broader reading public. Which is unconscionable: for, as the great mid-20th century Dutch historian Pieter Geyl has written, "The War of the Spanish Succession forms one of the most important episodes in modern history." In it, "decisions were made that helped make the world as we know

---

[12]Meyer's book is the best introduction to this aspect of Leibniz's thought.

it." The events which it showcased "are of an epic greatness."[13]

Geyl's estimate of that greatness is true as far as it goes. As he saw it, the war put a stop to Louis XIV's power grab and broke France as a hegemon in Europe, broke its capacity to bend Europe to its will. England was the great gainer, using this war as a springboard to European and global leadership.

This is true, but incomplete. The allies, including England, the Netherlands, and the various German states led by Austria and the Habsburg emperors (there were three during the war) did manage to keep France from achieving hegemony. But what was not achieved was the reaffirmation of institutions binding the nations of Europe as a *corpus Christianum*, sharing principles of order and justice, of dispersed sovereignty and the received constitution of Christendom, the fruit of a common Christian faith.[14]

Instead, the Treaty of Utrecht, the main treaty by which the war was concluded, furthered the conception of a world of every nation for itself, of autonomous states wielding absolute, centralized sovereignty – more so than the Peace of Westphalia, which is often seen as such a watershed. For what occurred here is that England and the Netherlands went their own ways, essentially pursuing a separate peace, culminating in the notorious Peace of Utrecht of 1713 (England, seeing the advantage to itself to be gained, was the ringleader here), leaving the major German states, Prussia and Austria, to do likewise. The smaller German states, which had worked feverishly to establish the imperial constitution on a sounder footing, saw their efforts came to nought.[15] And not only did the smaller states in

---

[13]Geyl, "Nederlands staatkunde in de Spaanse Successieoorlog," 77.

[14]Alvarado, *A Common Law* sheds further light on this constitution.

[15]Roger Wines, "The Imperial Circles, Princely Diplomacy, and Imperial Reform, 1681–1714," 1–29.

Germany suffer; the understanding of a pan-European Protestant fellowship was likewise offered up on the altar of one-
sided national sovereignty, turning Christianity into either a
purely national phenomenon (forms of Protestantism,
Gallicanism) or a virtually anti-national one (Ultramontan-
ism).[16] Religion became a domestic affair to be regulated by the
sovereign, used by him (or her) as an instrument to control the
populace, and thus, by association, in the end coming to par-
take of the opprobrium that increasingly became the monarch's lot. Nations no longer meddled in each other's domestic
affairs; the pan-European *corpus Christianum* was vanishing into
the mists.

It was then as it would later be at the Congress of Vienna in 1815: "I witness every day the astonishing tenacity with
which all the powers cling to the smallest points of separate
interest."[17] The time had come and gone that the Empire could
be set on a solid footing, able to provide an alternative to the
French free-thinking power-state. Austria was now free to pur-
sue dynastic interests rather than imperial ones; Prussia was
now free to impose itself as the power of the north. Holland
sunk back into pacifist lethargy; England pursued its overseas
colonial interests. And the spirit of humanistic autonomy took
hold.

The harbinger of things to come was the rise of Prussia
to Great Power status. Prince Eugene of Savoy, the general
leading the imperial armies against France and the Ottoman
Empire, once said that the ministers who counseled the emperor Leopold to grant the Duke of Brandenburg the status of
King of Prussia should have been hanged. Prussia often pur-

---

[16] Boles, *The Huguenots, the Protestant Interest, and the War of the Spanish
Succession, 1702-1714.*

[17] Castlereagh, quoted in Nicolson, *The Congress of Vienna,* 175.

sued its interests in the north to the detriment of the imperial way of life. Between Prussia and Austria, the Empire was torn apart. It was thus easy prey, when the time came, for revolutionary France.

The Revolution completed this long drawn-out process. By the late 18th century, monarchy had become anachronistic. In France, monarchy had taken the project of centralization about as far as it could; another form of regime had to come along to keep the process going. For the bottom line was not so much monarchy versus republic, although this was certainly at play; it was absolutism in lesser or greater degree.[18] This was the "calling" of France in world history. Therefore, the Revolution, or something like it – the replacement by some means of the absolute monarchy by an absolute popular government – had been foreordained by the events of a hundred years earlier. Had things turned out differently, France and its influence, extending beyond politics and military might to letters, religion, and culture, could have been hedged about, and the foundations of a Christian civilization of liberty under law more universally secured.

And so it came, the inevitable sequel to Meyer's "Seventeenth-Century Revolution." In the event, Prussia and Austria did manage to maintain their independence in the face of the Napoleonic conquest, although they had to forego significant chunks of territory, and make significant concessions, to do so. For its part, Bavaria, Stahl's birthplace, underwent an upheaval of enormous magnitude. Napoleon recognized a regime in Bavaria favorable to his rule and prepared to carry out reforms similar to the ones he himself had intro duced in

---

[18]"Though national sovereignty merely took the place of the princely sovereigns, it vastly intensified, as we know, the drive of Machiavellianism, extended it widely and made it all-inclusive." Schnabel, "The Bismarck Problem," 82.

Edmund Burke

France, most significantly the imposition of a general legal code, the famous *Code Civil.*

Revolutionary France, as de Tocqueville brilliantly surmised, simply furthered the work begun by French monarchs of yore.[19] The Revolution was merely an exchange of sovereign – the people for the king. The *form* of sovereignty – central government active in destroying all self-reliance and independence among the citizenry, making the citizens dependent upon itself – was left intact, and not only intact, but was perfected by being stripped of antiquated elements standing in the way of its perfection by bureaucratic administration.

The German states, on the other hand, had preserved more of the "original intent of the framers," so to speak, of the ancient constitution. What Edmund Burke had written of France applied even more to the German states[20]:

> You might, if you pleased, have profited of [the British] example, and have given to your recovered freedom a correspondent dignity. Your privileges, though discontinued, were not lost to memory. Your constitution, it is true, whilst you were out of possession, suffered waste and dilapidation; but you possessed in some parts the walls, and in all the foundations, of a noble and venerable castle. You might have repaired those walls; you might

---

[19]de Tocqueville, *The Old Regime and the French Revolution.*

[20]With this difference, that the Revolution was foisted on the German states, not generated internally.

have built on those old foundations. Your constitution was suspended before it was perfected; but you had the elements of a constitution very nearly as good as could be wished. In your old states you possessed that variety of parts corresponding with the various descriptions of which your community was happily composed.... Through that diversity of members and interests, general liberty had as many securities as there were separate views in the several orders; whilst by pressing down the whole by the weight of a real monarchy, the separate parts would have been prevented from warping and starting from their allotted places.[21]

Thus, despite the efforts of Napoleon, and before him the German princes that, with uneven results, had aped the court of Versailles, there was still a tenuous connection to the tradition of constitutional liberties. This memory served as the point of contact for the new philosophy of law and government first enunciated by Burke, the philosophy of conservatism.

Burke's philosophy constituted a frontal attack on the received wisdom of the Enlightenment, which to that point had enjoyed broad acceptance among the political elites of Europe. It was his *Reflections on the Revolution in France* that for the first time opened people's eyes to the true nature of the Revolution, to its radicalism and anti-Christian import. Burke exposed the doctrine of individual autonomy underlying the philosophy of natural rights, and which, he argued, served only to destroy God-given institutions in favor of an absolute, all-powerful state. For to make all authority subservient to the choice of the individual is to deny the naturalness, the rootedness, of all institutions incorporating authority from the family upward to the state, and extending to property as well as personal relations. Against this ideology, part and parcel of Meyer's "Sev-

---

[21]Burke, *Reflections*, 41.

enteenth Century Revolution," Burke argued that liberty is not a natural right in the sense of something existing prior to the formation of a polity; it is much rather an inheritance, something laboriously built up over generations of struggle. Burke's idea of progress was very much one of a progress in virtue, in the cultivation of liberty under law, the law-abiding and therefore liberty-loving citizen.

Burke's philosophy signaled the start of an anti-revolutionary movement that would continue to pick up steam, not least because of the spectacle provided by the French Revolution, which metastasized from a force for rebuilding the state into a force for destroying it. Increasingly, men of good will turned away from the philosophy that could generate such destruction, and opened their ears to Burke's argument.

In Germany, that argument came to be made most persuasively at the level of legal science. The imposition of the Napoleonic code called up a response in the form of a hearkening back to customary law as it had developed under Germany's native institutions. Friedrich Carl von Savigny, scion of a Huguenot family, pioneered the argument that law, like language, was not the product of a sovereign, created by the state and imposed on the populace. Law – like language – rather grew through custom and usage; it was a reflection of the character and aspirations of the nation; it could be studied, classified, and taught, but it could not be imposed or eliminated at will.

Savigny first put forward his argument in 1814, in a milestone entitled *The Vocation of Our Time for Legislation and Legal Science*. It was an important juncture, for the period of Napoleonic dominance was coming to an end. The Allied forces were closing in; the final victory at Waterloo was achieved shortly thereafter, in July 1815. It was time for the states of Germany, even revolutionary Bavaria, to pick up the pieces. The chief question would be, to what degree would the institu-

tions of the Revolution survive; to what degree would a
Burkean/Savignian conservatism gain hold; or was some
other alternative possible?

For the fall of Napoleon
spelled only the end of the
beginning as far as the Revolution was concerned. The
immediate threat was staved
off, but the potent elixir of
release from authority had
been tasted by the disenfranchised, and they would not
forget it.

Friedrich Carl von Savigny

But the princes, the ones who had endured such ignominy,
had been hounded from their positions, toppled from their
rightful places as leaders over the people, and as such were in
no mood to tolerate revolutionary notions once they were safe-
ly reensconced. The Congress of Vienna reestablished their
primacy. Led by Austrian foreign minister Clemens von
Metternich, the nations of Europe reacted to the Revolution
by formulating the principle of legitimism as the principle of
hereditary monarchy being the only form of lawful rule, entailing the restoration of those kings put out of power after 1789.
The conservative principles of Burke and Savigny here became
reduced to the notion of the maintenance of privilege and un-
trammeled monarchical rule as the only manner of government. Conservatism became reactionary; the principle of popular representation and participation in government became
submerged, where they would slumber, only to rise again, vio-
lently, to the surface.

This was the world into which Stahl was born. It was his

destiny to wrestle with the opposition of monarchy and revolution, to attempt to devise a solution upon the truly conservative principles pioneered by Burke and Savigny, to provide Germany with an alternative to reactionary privilege on the one hand and revolutionary democracy on the other. The problem was confounded by the fact that the institutions of Germany's inheritance had become thoroughly muddled and confused by the French example and the Napoleonic imposition. What still remained of a sound basis for the development of the institutions of liberty? Was anything left of those fabled German liberties? Was there even a healthy root remaining, upon which progressive institutions could be grafted?

2. Preparation

Friedrich Julius Stahl was born Julius Jolson (Joel's son) to Jewish parents on 16 January 1802, in the Bavarian town of Heidingsfeld. It was a propitious time to be born a Jew in Bavaria, for whatever else the Enlightenment brought in its train, it at least spelled some relief to non-Catholics from Counterreformation-inspired Catholic domination. Bavaria had been among the most closed of the Catholic German states; it was *Bavaria Sancta*, where all communication with the Protestant north was restricted and monitored, all literary activity subjected to the strictures of Catholic dogma. And the Jews of course were even more disenfranchised than the Protestants.

The Revolution hit Bavaria like a tidal wave. "Bavaria dropped out of the 17th into the 19th century without a transition."[22] A new ruler of the enlightened-despot persuasion, Max Joseph, acceded to the throne in 1799 and promptly pledged his full support to the revolutionary regime in Paris. Max Joseph's prime minister, the Count von Montgelas de Garnerin, was himself thoroughly imbued with the French spirit of centralization and bureaucracy. Montgelas initiated a policy of secularization aimed at removing the influence of the Catholic church from public life. The places of the priesthood and the monasteries in the estates were eliminated; church properties were expropriated; education was taken out of the hands of the church to be run by the state. The Christian confessions were placed on an equal, i.e., equally irrelevant, footing before the law.

Thus the idea of tolerance was imported into Bavaria.

---

[22]Masur, 12.

Tolerance was extended even to the Jews, who to this point had enjoyed precious little in the way of civil rights. The financial needs of the new regime necessitated a recourse to the Jewish community. The new policy did not extend to complete equality, but did entail access to public schools and the civil militia; the abolition of the *Leibzoll*, a special tax paid by Jews since the Middle Ages; the possibility of gaining citizenship; security of life and property; free choice of vocation; freedom of conscience; and, crucial to young Jolson, equal access to education.

These new decrees with regard to the Jews were slow to be put into effect across the Bavarian landscape, but they did take effect in the capital city, Munich, where Julius went to live with his grandfather, Abraham Uhlfelder, in 1808. The influence of Uhlfelder was formative to his entire future career. Uhlfelder was the leader of the Jewish community in Munich. He had been an agent and court factor – moneylender – to the King even back before Max Joseph had acceded to the Bavarian throne, when he was only the Elector of the Palatinate. Uhlfelder actively promoted the emergence of the Jews from the ghetto. For contrary to their position in Berlin, where Jews were among the leaders in social circles, in Munich they formed a tiny group, with neither synagogue nor graveyard. From his privileged position at court, Uhlfelder lobbied for the full access of Jews to public life, arguing for their fitness to shoulder the attendant responsibilities. His pioneering political activity powerfully impacted Julius, and must have inspired him in his own political career.

Julius was educated in the Jewish tradition, thus learning Hebrew and the Talmud. When the time came, he matriculated in the Wilhelm-Gymnasium, perhaps the most outstanding school in the country. Here he imbibed what he previously had observed from one remove, the spirit of German culture awakening from the shackles of French domination. He learned to appreciate another form of spirituality, one which was oriented more toward the combination of feeling and reason, embracing both the heart and the understanding, a spirituality in which the personal God reveals himself in the heart. He became acquainted with a Lutheranism that had not yielded to the rationalistic doctrine of the Enlightenment. He came into contact with the works of Goethe and Schiller, the latter causing Julius to consider that the Christian faith embodied a deeper truth than the fossilized religion of the Talmud. Although he left no record of how he in fact experienced the confrontation between the Christianity of his teachers and the faith of his fathers, it must have been a struggle for him; it was most certainly a conflict.

What is known is that he graduated from the gymnasium at the age of 17, excelling not only in "book learning" but also in music, as he developed into an accomplished violinist. He continued his studies in the classical and Christian tradition at the Lyceum, which in the Bavarian, Jesuit-inspired tradition came between gymnasium and university. After a seminar in figures from the classical tradition, such as Aeschylus, Pindar, Thucydides, Cicero, Horace, and Tacitus, he graduated in 1819. Next came a fateful step. The logical progression would be for him to matriculate at university, but Jews at this time were still excluded from institutions of higher learning. He decided to convert to Christianity, and, although here as in so many of such things the details are lacking, it is known that he successfully convinced his father that it was the right thing for him to do. That he did this out of conviction rather than convenience is demonstrated by the further course his life would take, a career of conviction and witness rather than convenience. Later, his entire family would follow in his footsteps.

For now, he moved to the city of Erlangen, a bulwark of

Lutheran piety, where he received instruction in the Lutheran - faith, and was baptized in November 1819, assuming the name by which he would become renowned throughout Europe, Friedrich Julius Stahl: Friedrich, after one of his teachers in Munich (the rationale behind the surname "Stahl" – German for steel – can only be surmised).

Stahl harbored no animosity towards his people or their religion. But besides having become a Christian, he had come to see himself as a German – the war of liberation against Napoleon had inspired in him patriotic feelings which he would carry with him his entire life[23] – and could not abide being kept apart in a separate nation, the utility of which, he had come to believe, had been fulfilled in the coming of Christ. Also, Stahl was fully accepted into his new community of faith.

Just prior to taking the step of baptism, Stahl found himself being ridiculed for it in a café frequented by students. As it happened, an acquaintance of his was present, to whom he turned for assistance. The gallant response brought the ridicule to a sudden halt. Stahl's vindicator was Freiherr Hermann von Rotenhan, a nobleman studying in Erlangen prior to assuming the responsibilities of the family estate. In Stahl's eyes, Von Rotenhan represented the ideal of German chivalry. The two's friendship would last their entire lives.

From Erlangen they both went to the Catholic university in Würzburg to study law. Here Stahl joined the *Burschenschaft*, a students' movement championing German patriotism. Stahl had grown up under the heady influence of the German liberation from the Napoleonic yoke. He was greatly impacted by it, and retained a streak of German patriotism which would stamp his political life. Speaking at the occasion of the second anniversary of the Würzburg chapter's establishment, Stahl extolled

---

[23]See 58 below.

the newfound values of German unity and liberty. Upon moving to Heidelberg to continue his law study, he was sent by the Heidelburg *Burschenschaft* to represent it at the national *Burschenschaft* assembly to be held – in secret – under the chairmanship of Von Rotenhan. The meeting revealed a split into two factions: one, including Stahl and Von Rotenhan, considered the *Burschenschaft* to be a Christian German youth movement intended to inculcate moral, scientific, and patriotic values; the other group viewed it as a political movement, the purpose of which was to foment change in government. Stahl argued that the purpose of the university was education, and that political action extended beyond the *Burschenschaft's* sphere of activity. Stahl's viewpoint prevailed. Here already, he demonstrated the rhetorical talent that one day would make him a leading figure in politics. And he would retain the spirit of German patriotism throughout his career.

To complete his legal studies Stahl in 1822 moved to Erlangen, where the spiritual atmosphere had gone from Enlightenment rationalism to a more pietistic, orthodox Lutheranism. He came under the influence of an evangelical Reformed professor, the students of whom, it was sometimes complained, were busier passing out tracts than pursuing their studies. Here, among other things, Stahl actively participated in debates over the abolition of dueling. He defended dueling, but only as a means toward defending one's honor; he rejected dueling as an end in itself, where defending one's honor is only an excuse to engage in it. He also joined the *Burschenschaft*, which however in Würzburg had continued with the radical approach that had been rejected at the national meeting. Stahl had no intention of going along with this approach; in fact, he wished to bring about the *Burschenschaft's* liquidation; but he was betrayed to the authorities. Participation in the *Burschenschaft* had been made a violation of the law. Stahl protested his innocence of any anti-

government activities, but it took nearly three years for him to
clear his name. In the meantime he was forced to suspend his
study at university.

These were certainly lean years for the young legal scholar.
In the forced hiatus, he busied himself chiefly with a struggle
with the philosophical system of Hegel, in particular the Hegelian legal philosophy. This rationalistic system had gotten
beyond natural rights individualism; Hegel took into account
the importance of social institutions as phenomena the establishment and justification of which lay beyond the mere consent of the members. Thus the Hegelian system answered one
of the chief complaints raised against Enlightenment rationalism, that it exclusively relied on the individual will and individual choice as its ultimate justifying claim. This also explains the
attraction of Hegel to conservative thinkers then (and now, for
that matter). But Hegel's system was pantheistic, and resolved
all phenomena into *a priori* logical categories. This would of
course prove unacceptable to Stahl, but he nevertheless wres-
tled with Hegel so as to distill the positive elements which
would prove fruitful in his own work.

After finally restoring his position, Stahl returned to Würzburg, where he quickly gained his doctorate with a dissertation
on Roman law. He subsequently took a position as an unpaid
faculty member (*privatdozent*) of the newly formed department
of law at the University of Munich. The influence of the Historical School as developed by Savigny was already becoming
clear in his work. In Munich Stahl was able to attend the lectures of the great contemporary philosopher Schelling, which
helped him to overcome the rationalistic influence of Hegel.
Schelling's philosophy was oriented about the personal God,
which helped Stahl to nail down a philosophical grounding for
his theological convictions.

Having overcome the influence of Hegel, Stahl was ready to

formulate his own, orthodox Christian, philosophy of law. He was not slow to realize this project, in 1829 publishing the first volume of his *Philosophy of Law*, entitled *The History of Legal Philosophy*.[24] It was a path-breaking effort, incorporating his conviction that either Christ stood above science, or science stood above Christ – there was no middle way. The approach of the Historical School, and of Edmund Burke, gained a ringing endorsement, while also receiving needed criticism on the basis of Christian theology.

The Achilles' heel of the Historical School had been its lack of a solid philosophical grounding. What is it that justified a historical legacy? What made tradition something to be valued and maintained, beyond the sheer force of habit? In opposition to the natural rights school of the Enlightenment and the French Revolution, Savigny, following Burke, had argued that social institutions are evolved rather than created; they rest on habit and custom rather than rational deliberation and decree. But hadn't even Pope Gregory VIII argued that Christ didn't say He was the custom, but that He was the Truth? Custom in and of itself provides no final justification.

Stahl grounded the justification for the methodology of the Historical School squarely in the Christian revelation. He argued that God works *through* cultures and civilizations to realize His will. He works *through* persons who nevertheless operate in terms of their own wills; and He orchestrates their work, as the Supreme Will. He exercises His will over man by making that will known in the form of moral commands and strictures; man puts these imperatives into effect through the structures of earthly life. And the structures of earthly life, such as the family, the city, the nation, are not mere artifacts of human

---

[24]I follow Masur's description of the book because he refers exclusively to the first edition, access to which I did not have.

will. They find their ultimate source in the divine will, who has also established their constitutions. These institutions therefore stand above the mere wills of the members. "Church and State, family and marriage do not arise from individual upwellings, private goals and intentions, like human creations based in agreement or contract, but as the God willed, moral-legal fulfillment and ordering of needs. In this manner, legal ordinances grow up into institutions which first derive their full significance and supra-human value from God's plan for the human race."[25]

As Masur argues, here is where Stahl showed the benefit of his study of Hegel. But Stahl managed to avoid the either/or of Enlightenment individualist rationalism on the one hand and Hegelian whole-oriented, pantheistic rationalism on the other. Stahl made neither the individual nor the whole the ordering principle of his system. "He begins neither with the isolated individual of the Social Contract, nor with the Whole that is more than the sum of its parts, but from both, establishing over them the construct of the social world, by accounting for the inseparable functional coherence in which they stand."[26]

It was Stahl's unshakeable conviction that law could not be deducted straight from universal principles of logic, but much rather that it must be viewed at the level of the actual conditions in which it arises and exists. This ground-level realism is not however enough; it must be combined with the normative order of God's requirements. Legal institutions are the result. They stand as a power over the will, while also being the result of human action. They mediate the will of God without being the direct expression of it. It is the combination of wills which

---

[25]Masur, 120.
[26]Masur, 120.

is key here, as this is Stahl's view of the kingdom: it is the rule over free wills. Through His commands and through his creative will which has established the nature and intention of the various social institutions, God has provided a framework within which human society can evolve. And in fact history is moving towards a goal. Not the fulfillment of the kingdom of God on earth, but the preparation for it. The law which undergirds and structures human society is thus the servant of God's kingdom, enabling it to flourish, without itself being that kingdom's fulfillment, it being an external, coercive order.

History is moving towards a future; it is not purposeless. The works of previous generations live on into the present. "The past, says Stahl in a striking formulation, is not merely passing; it is the immanent cause of the present. It [i.e., the present – RCA] is as the past, as still containing in it what it was. Through all of history a transmission of inner culture and external conditions occurs from generation to generation, from people to people. Every age is to build on it according to its own special gift as a work that it did not begin and that it will not complete."[27] Every age and every people receives what it is from the past as an inheritance which it is to improve upon. This is the foundational principle of the Historical School and of Stahl's legal philosophy. Its contingent nature is self-evident. Both in the inheritance and in the improvement lie imperfections and failures as well as achievements and progress. It all occurs under the watchful eye of God and in accordance with His higher will.

It is remarkable that Stahl was able to complete and publish this book, considering the personal situation he faced. His father had recently passed away, and, he being the eldest, care for his many underage brothers and sisters now fell to him. In

---

[27]Masur, 126.

providing for their needs there were days when he ate nothing but potatoes.[28] Initial requests for paid professorships fell on deaf ears. Stahl turned to journalism, becoming the editor of the "Friend of the Throne and the People," the crown's official publication. There he did his best to defend royal policy while maintaining objectivity. But he came away unsatisfied with his efforts. He became convinced that the path forward was not simply to defend the crown but also to appropriate the truth and the good in what the proponents of popular sovereignty were advocating. A synthesis had to be found between monarchy and republicanism, and Stahl meant to achieve it.

Finally the professorship he so desired fell to him. The University of Würzburg took him on as a full professor. Although this brought an end to his financial problems, it did face him with a degree of isolation, as Würzburg was a Catholic university. During his period at Würzburg Stahl busied himself mainly in completing the second volume of his *Philosophy of Law*. The first had combined the history of legal philosophy with a presentation of Stahl's own philosophy. He now split these two into separate books, publishing the expanded versions.

In the meantime, like-minded professors in Erlangen who had been working to gain for him a position on the faculty at their university succeeded in doing so in 1834. He was appointed professor of constitutional and ecclesiastical law, and became one of the leading figures on campus.

At Erlangen Stahl was able to complete the *Philosophy of Law* with the third part (actually, the second part of the second volume), on constitutional law, which was published in 1837. Here already were contained the doctrines he would expound

---

[28]Masur, 251.

through all his years of university and political activity.

Stahl formulated a theory of constitutionalism based on the received Germanic traditions centered in monarchy but which went beyond the simple conception of the crown as the isolated sovereign. The constitution prescribed the rights and duties of both crown and assembly – there could be no question of the rights of sovereignty being the personal possession of the monarch. In this, Stahl went beyond the conservatism of his day. His decisive exposition in favor of a truly public, overarching state order, in which office and law prescribed and bounded sovereignty, constituted a great step forward for German conservatism. It also decisively opposed the parliamentarianism of the liberals, who wished to hollow out the crown's rights of sovereignty. Stahl saw in this the attempt to remove the expression of Christian religion in public life.

The chief motivation behind Stahl's advocacy of monarchy was that it was indispensable, in his view, to maintaining Christianity as the public confession of faith. As he would put it later in life, in a letter to Von Rotenhan:

> It is precisely in the people that there is now resistance and struggle against Christianity, while among the princes (partly from the heart, partly from prudence) the tendency is to maintain the faith. This is the main reason why I, without abandoning a political doctrine or conviction, see myself impelled toward the side of monarchy. If the assemblies had had sole decision-making power, we would long ago have fully de-Christianized the state and perhaps already have begun persecuting true Christians.[29]

Although the *Philosophy of Law* was received favorably by Savigny and other representatives of the Historical School, it

---

[29]Koglin, 344.

was not spared criticism. Schelling, for one, made sure to distance himself from Stahl; he did not want people to think that Stahl, who had attended Schelling's lectures in Munich, somehow was expounding his views. Interestingly, conservative critics in Berlin accused Stahl of being a pantheist, believing that they detected Hegelianism in his philosophy. But the Hegelians themselves could not abide him either – his was the first criticism of rationalism from a Christian viewpoint.[30]

During this period, Stahl found the woman with whom he would share the rest of his life. Julie Kindler was the daughter of a shoemaker – Stahl's colleagues were surprised that he would marry "beneath his condition." But he had found a woman who would complement him well. Julie was above all practical and had good sense – something which Stahl, the proverbial absent-minded professor, had need of.[31] She was vivacious, full of life, and most of all shared a fervent faith in Jesus Christ. When later in life they moved in circles of power in Berlin, Julie found amused acceptance as her manners were considered typically Bavarian; she not having much of a mind for fashion, Bismarck once poked fun at her "marvelous dress."[32] For her, Julius was her "little man," [mein kleiner Mann]; her respect, care and concern for him, through his frequent bouts of poor health, shine through her letters.[33]

His appointment to Erlangen came at a propitious time. Despite the decree establishing equal rights between Christian confessions in Bavaria, the crown was beginning to push a

---

[30]Von Arnim, xxii-xxiii.

[31]In a letter to Bismarck later in life, Stahl complained that he could not pass on a copy of a book he had recommended, because "what is my personal fate, I could not find it anymore." Koglin, 374.

[32]Quoted in Fafié, 26.

[33]Examples of which are contained in Koglin.

pro-Catholic policy that financially disadvantaged the University of Erlangen, Bavaria's only Protestant university.[34] Furthermore, Lutheranism was experiencing an evangelical revival, centered in Erlangen, and the believing professors there were central to this revival. Stahl and his group of like-minded professors across various disciplines all rejected Hegelianism and worked to minimize its influence at the university. They participated in Bible studies and even established hand laborers' associations in which they actively worked to pass on a Christian vision of culture. These efforts were viewed with suspicion by the crown, which in particular considered such associations of the working class to be breeding grounds of sedition. Laws were passed restricting these efforts, even though they were conducted in a strictly a-political manner. And it was not only a reactionary Catholicism that inspired this opposition; the spirit of secular rationalism issuing from the so-called "Friends of Light" (*Lichtfreunde*) was also at work.[35]

By this time Stahl had become a figure of some reputation. He was therefore appointed by the university to represent it at the Bavarian assembly. The assembly was composed from five electorates: landed aristocrats exercising local judicial authority, universities, clergy, cities and "markets," and landowners. Many of the delegates, such as the 29 innkeepers and beerbrewers, were political novices who scarcely participated in debates. The actual business was mainly conducted by about 30 delegates.[36]

---

[34]The following discussion of Stahl's political activity in Bavaria owes much to Füßl, 69 ff.

[35]There is an informative chapter on the Friends of Light in Bigler, *The Politics of German Protestantism*, ch. 6.

[36]Füßl, 83.

Here Stahl once again came into contact with his friend Von Rotenhan, who formed part of the aristocratic faction. Stahl quickly gained the confidence of his fellow Protestant parliamentarians and was appointed to various committees. He proved himself decisive, articulate, considered, brave, and confident. And beyond that, impartial.

This was crucial. Stahl's impartiality entailed that although he was a supporter of monarchy, he did not agree with all crown policy. This was obviously the case with regard to the promotion of Catholicism; it also extended to defending the assembly's rights where they were infringed by the crown.

This became evident in a debate about the crown's right to dispose of budget surpluses. The crown argued that it could do what it pleased with these surpluses; the assembly argued that its right to approve taxes entailed some say in how surplus tax revenues should be applied. Stahl's position was to adhere to a strict interpretation of the Bavarian constitution, and thus to respect the rights of both crown and assembly. Even this went too far for King Ludwig, who personally held Stahl accountable for obstructing his will. Ludwig therefore had Stahl dismissed from his position as professor of constitutional law, having him assigned to the professorship of procedural law, which lay outside of Stahl's area of expertise. This was done not only to hit at a defender of the rights of the assembly, but also at a representative of political Protestantism.[37] Stahl felt the wound deeply; he would refuse his university's later call to represent it at the next session of the assembly. But he had been able to put the principles developed in his *Philosophy of Law* into action, and experience the effect.

Having withdrawn from politics, Stahl now had more time

---

[37]Masur, 292.

to devote to his studies. He was able to put together a study on the constitution of the church: *The Church Constitution According to the Doctrine and Law of the Protestants* (Erlangen, 1840). This work was intended to highlight the distinctive nature of the church as perceived by Protestants over against Bavaria's prevailing Catholicism, while also suggesting improvement of the existing Protestant church order.

Church organization was an area that Stahl felt Protestantism had neglected. The Protestant church order had been conceived mainly in opposition to the Roman Catholic one, focusing on the church as the communion of saints, the "priesthood of believers," in which the gospel is taught in its purity and the sacraments properly administered, while downplaying the "organic" side of the church, its institutional framework. Stahl countered by emphasizing the role of the office in the church, and with his emphasis on the personal nature of rule, he argued in favor of an episcopalian system in which bishops represent the institution over against the congregations. This he felt would provide the best safeguard for the purity of doctrine.

There must be a higher legitimation of order than the mere consent of the governed: of this Stahl was convinced, and he wished to see this principle expressed not only in the state but in the church as well. The foundational pillars of the church, he argued, were constitution and confession, both of which stood over, and conditioned, the will of the members.

For this reason he distinguished between the church and the congregation. The church is an institution established by God.

In opposition to the Protestantism of his time, which viewed the church as the congregation and the congregation as the church, Stahl put forward the concept of the transpersonal institution, under the dominion of which all human common life takes place. The continued existence of the church is that of an organized institution; it lives as a higher power over men. As well, the church for Stahl is a spiritual gathering of souls, and thus a gathered community. But it is not merely a gathered community, it is also a gathering institution.... For Stahl, the community is merely an activity towards God, while the church is an activity in God's omnipotence towards men; the community is the embodiment of currently living people, the church is the continued historical existence through all times.[38]

As a corollary to this understanding of institution vs. congregation, Stahl viewed the role of the congregation in the church order as mainly a negative one. The congregation has the right of appropriation, cooperation, and resistance, not the right of church government. The main role in church government is reserved to the clergy, consistent with Stahl's episcopalian predilections.

It must be said that part of the reason Stahl desired to restrict the role of the congregation in church government is that he wished to erect a dike against the revolutionary tendencies so visibly at work in 19th century Germany, tendencies which vitiated the movement toward popular participation in government. Congregationalism in Germany had imbibed this revolutionary tendency, and was striving not simply for greater participation but for the overthrow of authority altogether, extending even to the authority of Scripture. Theological liberalism had allied with political liberalism. Stahl's view was that the congregation would be ready for a greater role when the contemporary apostasy had been overcome, and motivation for

---

[38]Masur, 320.

church renewal was tapped from a Christian root.[39]

Stahl also argued for the independence of the church over against the state. He saw three main failings in the conception of church and state, corresponding to the three main confessions in Germany. First, the tendency to sacrifice the independence of the state and allow it to be absorbed into the church: this was the failing of the Roman Catholic church. Second, there was the tendency to absorb the church into the state: this was the Lutheran weakness. Third, the tendency to separate church and state: this is where the Reformed church was weak. For Stahl, the church could not be separated from the state; the state must be a Christian state. Church and state are two separate, independent institutions, but nonetheless stand in the closest mutual relation. The state is a mere earthly institution, and is a vague reflection of the power and majesty of the eternal kingdom. It will pass away with the earthly conditions upon which it rests. The church, on the other hand, is destined for eternity; it will transition into the eternal kingdom, and in fact inwardly already embodies the eternal kingdom. Church and state are both God-established institutions set over man to guide him on his way to his eternal destiny, but each with its own specific role to play; neither is to usurp the role of the other.[40]

If Stahl's work on the philosophy of law made a splash, the publication of his book on the church spawned a tidal wave. It was everywhere the subject of discussion, both in a positive and negative sense. Predictably, the members of the Historical School were favorable, the Hegelians and liberals antagonistic. "When one reviews the passionate reaction that Stahl's thin

---

[39]Masur, 323.
[40]Masur, 326.

book generated on all fronts... one must conclude that the times were ripe for the renewed discussion of the entire issue. Stahl's work had the effect of a spark on a pile of explosives."[41]

The book also caught the eye of the crown prince of Prussia, the future Friedrich Wilhelm IV. It was enough to inspire him to invite Stahl to assume the chair of ecclesiastical and constitutional law at the University of Berlin. In fact, when he ascended to the throne in 1840 upon the death of his father, his first act with regard to carrying out his vision of renewal of church and state was to appoint Stahl to the university. By this time Stahl had made his name as a professor, as an intellectual, and as a politician, albeit on the small stage of Bavaria. He would now have the opportunity to work to implement his vision on the stage of Prussia, Germany's leading Protestant state. He would be able to join forces with the conservatives gathered about Friedrich Wilhelm's throne. The future looked bright. But appearances can be deceiving.

---

[41]Masur, 329.

3. The Calm Before the Storm

Stahl arrived at the University of Berlin with a reputation having preceded him – that of a reactionary "pietist" and "absolutist." His first lecture gave an indication of what he could expect from his new academic home. In it, he developed the contrast between the Historical School and the natural law school of legal philosophy. His attack on natural law incited the Hegelians who were present to make their contrasting opinions felt. They began to make loud noises and scuff their shoes on the floor, in order, as Stahl put it, "to make it impossible for me to continue, or to embarrass me." One of those present reported that briefcases, books, and umbrellas were hurled against the lectern, forcing Stahl to beat a retreat. This report is probably exaggerated; Stahl apparently brought the disturbance to a halt by responding: "Sirs, *I* am here to *teach, you* are here to *listen.* Judgements you may make at home; here, however, you must not disturb the order and peace."[42]

Despite the fact that he enjoyed the king's favor – or perhaps precisely because of that favor – Stahl had the deck stacked against him. "A significant odium hangs over me here," he wrote to his friend, Rudolph Wagner, in a letter dated 1 January 1841. "Everywhere there is an excitement of emotion against alleged pietism and one fears its being favored by the king. My appointment is not the least disapproved act." It was felt, wrote Stahl, that he owed his appointment solely to the king's favor. "Although it stemmed from Savigny and the

---

[42]For this account, see Füßl, pp. 110-111. Julie Stahl provides a more wide-ranging report of this incident and of Stahl's first days at the University of Berlin: Koglin, 236ff.

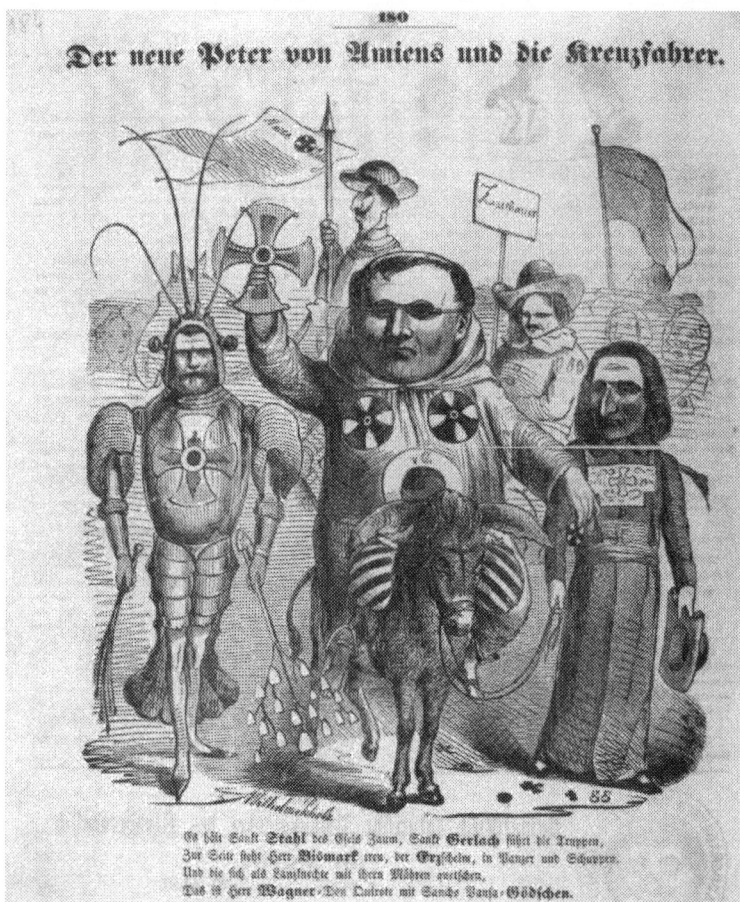

180

Der neue Peter von Amiens und die Kreuzfahrer.

Es hält Sankt **Stahl** des Esels Zaun, Sankt **Gerlach** führt die Truppen,
Zur Seite steht Herr **Bismark** treu, der **Erzschelm**, in Panzer und Schuppen.
Und die sich als Lanzknechte mit ihren Mähren quetschen,
Das ist Herr **Wagner**-Don Quixote mit Sancho Pansa-**Gödschen.**

"The new Peter of Amiens and the Crusaders." Bismarck on the left, Ludwig von Gerlach in the middle, Stahl on the right caricatured as a Jesuit father with hook nose and sunken cheeks. *Kladderadatsch* satirizes the new conservative publication, the *Kreuzzeitung* (see p. 42 below).

faculty, with the king only lending his enthusiastic support, it is put solely to the latter's account."[43]

The liberals never considered him to be anything but a reactionary, a member of the "extreme right," something which he

---

[43]Koglin, 240.

vehemently disputed. As he wrote to his friend Von Rotenhan, "that explains why one considers me a champion of the extreme right, which indeed I am not."[44] For their part, the conservatives viewed him as being too open to constitutional reform, too little attached to the cause of monarchical majesty. Add to this his Jewish background, which was never forgotten. One leading conservative confessed that in his "general antipathy against everything coming from Israelites" he had "not taken the least notice of any of Stahl's books."[45] The liberals made fun of his Jewish ethnicity: "caricatures in the *Kladderadatsch* [the Prussian equivalent of *Punch* – RCA] pictured Stahl with a pronounced hook nose and protruding cheek bones."[46]

Friedrich Wilhelm went ahead with his plans to call a general synod, which took place in June 1846. Almost from the start the synod headed off in the wrong direction. For instance, various Prussian city authorities requested the synod to carry out liberal reforms, which of course embittered the monarch who wished to restore the original purity of the church. He responded to the provocation by insisting that he also wished for the church to reform itself, but that "it should do so not by following the path of false freedom but rather by following the path of lawful freedom. It cannot be reformed on the basis of new or arbitrary teachings, but only on the basis of our ancient faith, upon which the whole Church of Christ has been built, and which has been established for all time."[47]

Stahl was chosen to represent the legal faculty of the Uni-

---

[44]Koglin, 344.
[45]Cf. Füßl, 111.
[46]*Ibid.*, n19.
[47]Quoted in Barclay, 95.

versity of Berlin at the synod. In one area, his contribution was crucial to the course the synod took. In the constitutional question, one of the two main issues the synod tackled, Stahl acted as expert adviser. In that capacity he submitted a draft embodying a middle way, combining elements from both the consistorial and the synodal forms of government, the two forms then in existence in the Prussian churches: the eastern provinces maintained the consistorial form, the western [Rhenish-Westphalian] provinces the synodal, corresponding to the Lutheran-Reformed divide.[48]

Stahl developed his position in line with *The Church Constitution According to the Doctrine and Law of the Protestants* (see p. 29 above). Here, however, in accordance with the practical nature of the subject, he left off of proposing an episcopalian church order, although he did make mention of his "episcopalian tendencies." He structured his argument in terms of the two poles as put forward in *The Church Constitution*, "church" being the God-established institution and "congregation" being the man-formed community of believers. The congregational pole is maintained by the development of a presbyterian, synodal structure along the lines of Reformed church government; the churchly pole is furthered by the recognition of the Word of God and the evangelical confession as the foundation of the church and standard of church government. The establishment of a supreme consistory, the requirement that members of the consistory submit to the standards of the church, and an emphasis on the importance of superintendents and general superintendents were also recommended. The congregational character preserves the church from hierarchy; the churchly

---

[48]Nabrings, 128ff.

character, from profanation.[49]

Stahl viewed the presbyterian form of government as going a long way toward realizing these principles in practice. The presbyterian form recognized the Word of God as an authority over and above the will of the members. According to it, this Word along with the creeds and confessions are the basis for public doctrine. As he put it, the presbyterial form is "a noble form of deep Christian meaning [Sinnes]." Nevertheless, it was not perfect: it insufficiently embodied the "churchly" principle. In the absence of an episcopal element, the presbyterian form needed supplementation in the form of a stable element, which could be provided by the consistorial form of government. In this way the consistorial element could provide a positive contribution without falling back into the error of the state exercising authority in the church.[50]

Clearly Stahl was putting forward a compromise; understandably, his proposal was criticized from both sides. Defenders of the consistorial form wished to preserve the prince's leadership role in the church, while synodal defenders wished to place leadership in the hands of the synod itself. His proposal nevertheless was accepted as the majority view. On Stahl's recommendation, the majority further proposed that a supreme consistory be established to have oversight over matters of doctrine, liturgy and worship.[51] On the other hand, Stahl opposed a proposed rule of ordination after initially supporting it, having come to the conclusion that it undermined the Augsburg Confession.[52]

---

[49]Nabrings, 157.
[50]Nabrings, 156.
[51]Nabring, 128-129.
[52]Nabring, 129-130.

The synod's work ended up incurring the opprobrium of Friedrich Wilhelm, who rejected both the mixed constitution of synod and consistory and the new rule of ordination.[53] One recommendation Friedrich Wilhelm did eventually act on was the one calling for the establishment of a supreme consistory. This was accomplished early in 1848. For the rest, this period signified a high-water mark in Stahl's willingness to compromise on issues of church government. And after the dam burst in 1848, Stahl saw his position increasingly being shunted aside in favor of unification through dilution.

In fact, it is now time to cross the threshold. For Germany had been living in a period of false security; the storms of revolution were brewing. The *Vormärz* (pre-March) period, as historians have dubbed it, was coming to an end. March 1848 was coming, and with it events that would forever alter the course of German history.

---

[53]Barclay, 95-96. Barclay, basing his view on second-hand reports, argues that Friedrich Wilhelm "loathed" the synodal church order and was "horrified" at the synod's recommendation partially to introduce it across Prussia. However Stahl, who enjoyed the king's confidence in such matters, was the one who actually proposed this step. Certainly Stahl was proposing a compromise and not the kind of church order he envisioned in his book of 1840. But it is somewhat difficult to imagine that he would propose something so offensive to the king, if in fact it was so offensive.

4. Into the Breach

Friedrich Wilhelm on 11 April 1847 convoked the long-expected national assembly, the United Diet. It was not popularly elected, but rather was composed of delegates from the provincial estates, themselves the products of severely restricted electorates. As well, its remit was severely restricted; it would have the power to approve or reject requests by the government for new loans, new taxes, or increases in taxes. As such, it was viewed by liberals with dismay, and many seriously considered a boycott. Conservatives for their part viewed the venture with foreboding. It was a new departure for Prussia, which had never experienced national assemblies. Conservatives feared it would open a door to the eventual conquest of the state by proponents of the Revolution and popular sovereignty.[54]

Right from the start, Friedrich Wilhelm made it clear that he would not allow the country to move in the direction of a written constitution and shared sovereignty. As he put it in his opening address to the assembly: "No power of the earth will succeed in moving Me to transform that natural relationship between ruler and people… into a legalistic or constitutional one; and that I will never ever allow a written piece of paper to come between Our Lord God in Heaven and this country… to rule us with its paragraphs as a substitute for our old, sacred loyalty." In fact, he argued, "The Christian people [of Prussia], that simple true, loyal people, does not want representatives to share in government; it does not want sovereignty to be di-

---

[54]Barclay, 126-128.

vided, or to see the genuine power of its kings broken."[55]

This was, of course, not what the majority of delegates wanted to hear. Prussian educated opinion was with the liberals, and the Diet could only serve to disappoint. Not surprisingly, the speech "hit the assembly like a thunderbolt.... With one blow the *Stände* [estates – RCA] have seen their hopes and desires obliterated; not one happy face left the assembly."[56] The Diet chafed under a purview restricted to matters of taxation; and as it was not pleased, it reciprocated by refusing to fund a planned rail link between Berlin and Königsberg. The king "had assumed that the Diet's principal function was to discuss loans and other financial affairs, and nothing more. In fact, however, it devoted most of its attention to constitutional matters."[57]

Pressure for constitutional reforms continued to build, not only in Prussia but all across Europe. Matters reached a head in February of 1848, when revolution broke out in France, toppling the so-called July Monarchy of Louis-Philippe and establishing the Second Republic. This was the signal agitators in Berlin and elsewhere had been awaiting.[58]

Skirmishes between demonstrators and troops began in earnest on March 18. The government was in total confusion, with no one, least of all Friedrich Wilhelm, sure of what course to take. Seeing the writing on the wall, Friedrich Wilhelm had been spending the last few months feverishly considering and proposing the kind of reforms he had rejected out of hand

---

[55]Quoted in Barclay, 128.

[56]Count Trauttmansdorff to Metternich, 16 April 1847, quoted in Barclay, 128-129.

[57]Barclay, 130.

[58]The following narrative mainly follows Barclay, 138ff.

only a year earlier. Now it was too late. There were but two avenues of action available; either withdraw from the city, surround it with troops, and blast it into submission, or have the troops return to their barracks and hope the citizenry would come to its senses.

Having chosen the latter course, Friedrich Wilhelm issued his famous "To My Dear Berliners" letter, ascribing the bloodshed already committed to misunderstanding and the action of a group of rioters. He pleaded with the citizens to abandon the barricades, in exchange for which he would order the immediate backdown of troops.

As the citizens digested this latest development, the commander of the army in Berlin ordered his men to return to their barracks. Not only that: the palace guard likewise abandoned their posts, something Friedrich Wilhelm had had no intention of letting happen. The palace was left to the citizens, only that Friedrich Wilhelm and the queen were left in it!

In short order, an armed "Citizens' Guard" took control of the palace. There followed a series of humiliating concessions. The king and queen were forced to pay homage, the king cap in hand, to those who had died in the street fighting; the queen, "white with fear and horror," remarked that "the only thing missing now is the guillotine."[59] Prussia's first constitutional government was announced. And to cap it all, Friedrich Wilhelm rode on horseback through the streets of Berlin draped in the black, red, and gold flag of the German national movement, issuing a declaration that he would henceforth take the lead in promoting pan-German unity: "Prussia will be subsumed into Germany," he proclaimed.

This was astounding. Friedrich Wilhelm had now proved

---

[59]Quoted in Barclay, 145.

Ludwig von Gerlach

willing to seek to heal the wounds, the gaping holes, in the Prussian social and political fabric by wrapping himself in the flag of pan-Germanism. Royalist conservatives were aghast. Such a program could only be pursued at the expense of good relations with Austria, which along with Russia was one of the three members of the Holy Alliance that since 1815 had championed the cause of monarchy against revolution. Pan-Germanism entailed the serious threat not only of incurring the wrath of both Austria and Russia, but also of helping the parliamentarians into the saddle. It enjoyed the approval of the liberals only because they believed it would bring about the elimination of the separate monarchies and establish representative government in their place. Could such an ideal be made serviceable to Friedrich Wilhelm's avowed conservatism? Or was he delivering a hostage to fortune?

In the meantime, the conservatives in Berlin, including Stahl, for a time abandoned the capital in an attempt to regroup and come up with a strategy to deal with the changed political realities. Two concrete developments came out of this: the establishment of a new conservative journal, the famed *Neuen Preußischen Zeitung*, nicknamed the *Kreuzzeitung* (Cross-Journal) after the cross printed on the masthead; and the formation of the so-called "Camarilla," a group of conservatives with unofficial connections to the king who worked to shape policy behind the scenes, sideskirting the actual cabinet and government. Both of these developments were manifestations of the fact that conservatives were beginning to take on the shape of a coherent party.

Stahl became a frequent contributor to the *Kreuzzeitung*, and although not a member of the Camarilla, he had close ties to its members. His relationship with Ludwig von Gerlach, one of the leaders of the Prussian conservatives and a future political martyr for the cause of Christendom, was especially important. The two future leaders of the conservative party learned much from each other: Gerlach of the value of constitutional monarchy, and Stahl of the Prussian tradition as a valuable one within the broader German-Christian heritage:

> Von Gerlach himself explains that since my document concerning "The Monarchical Principle" he has become convinced of my viewpoint and of the one-sidedness of Haller's [patrimonial monarchical viewpoint – RCA]. In exchange I have received much from him, especially since 1848, not so much contradicting my previous viewpoint as partly supplementing it, partly providing something new. Namely, the nerves of the Prussian state, the tradition of this country, the specific Prussiandom which he so energetically represents is so allied to my entire historical conception, that it has come about that in ten years I have gone through so much with Prussia, jointly experienced so much, jointly struggled, that I truly feel that this is my fatherland.[60]

In the event, the government managed to restore order in Berlin. But Friedrich Wilhelm had paid a price: he had called for the convocation of a new national assembly, this time one on a pan-German basis. Prussia would henceforth be subsumed in Germany, he had proclaimed; now he had to back it up.

The Union Assembly, charged with establishing a government and drawing up a constitution for the united Germany,

---

[60]Stahl to Rotenhan, in Koglin, 343.

gathered for the first time in Frankfurt's St. Paul's church on 18 May. Without consulting the princes of the constituent states, the assembly elected Archduke John of Austria as "Regent of the Empire" [*Reichsverweser*] and established a provisional central authority, the first collective German representative institution since the dissolution of the Holy Roman Empire. This so-called "professors' parliament" then turned to the business of writing up a comprehensive bill of fundamental rights, entirely in line with the spirit of the times. A new Germany was taking shape.

For their part, the conservatives flailed around trying to figure out which course to take. That is, apart from Stahl, who for years had been preparing for this very moment. It was his cohorts in the conservative movement that were caught by surprise. He need not feverishly adapt his position to new realities; his position had already been hammered out over years of deliberation in engagement with the issues and movements of the day and the ultimate foundations underlying them.

> Stahl's conservative program gained in value [in the eyes of contemporary conservatives – RCA] because it was formulated, not as a concession to the liberal constitutional movement under pressure from the revolution, but rather... on the basis of Stahl's own requirements, already raised before the revolution. In 1845 the monarchical powers could not come to terms with Stahl's constitutional ideal. Now, under pressure from revolutionary developments, they recognized its justification and necessity, albeit often grudgingly.[61]

While the pan-German constitutional debate was taking place in Frankfurt and the Prussian monarchy was regrouping,

---

[61]Füßl, 134.

Stahl in September was attending the first annual Protestant national church assembly, held in Wittenberg, over which he co-presided. The assembly was heavily influenced by the outside political debate regarding national unification. Many delegates championed the unification of the Protestant churches as a step on the way to political unification; on the other hand, others championed church unification as a means to support existing governments. Furthermore, the assembly was seen as a means of enabling the church to gain more independence from the state. For his part, Stahl championed a confederational approach safeguarding the existing churches' independence. He also argued, in support of a motion from Ludwig von Gerlach, that the assembly should declare its opposition to the spirit of the Revolution. His advice went unheeded, as many liberal-minded participants viewed this as an unacceptable mingling of church and state. Stahl argued that the issue was quite properly a matter of Christian ethics rather than mere politics.[62]

In Prussia, meanwhile, the Berlin assembly – which had been called at the same time as the Frankfurt national assembly – had been putting together a proposed constitution for Prussia. As the assembly adopted one liberal proposition after another, a head-on collision with the king was only a matter of time. The assembly attempted to cashier officers from the army who had worked against the revolution; it demanded that the army swear an oath to support the "Regent of the Empire" and concurrently replace the Prussian black and white cockade with its pan-German black-red-gold counterpart.[63] The straw that broke the camel's back was the assembly's removal of any

---

[62]Nabrings, 131ff; Füßl, 140ff.
[63]Dietrich, *Kleine Geschichte Preußens*, 167.

mention of the king's office as existing by the grace of God. After dismissing his rather liberal-minded government, Friedrich Wilhelm found ministers who would maintain a hard line. The new minister-president, Count Brandenburg, in November removed the assembly to another city, and on December 5 dissolved it for good.[64]

This was, as Schoeps puts it, a coup d'etat, as the king had no right to dissolve the assembly.[65] But Friedrich Wilhelm followed it up with the promulgation of a new constitution. In this he was greatly helped by Stahl, who also helped to draft the king's version.[66] The new constitution incorporated many of the proposals originally made by the Berlin assembly, so as to assuage affronted minds and facilitate the constitution's acceptance. The core of the new constitution was the establishment of direct elections, extending the vote to all adult males except those on poor relief, albeit for the lower house; suffrage with respect to the upper house was restricted to those with significant means. In this, Friedrich Wilhelm had made good on his proclamation of March 22. He proclaimed the constitution by royal patent on the same day as he dissolved the assembly, on December 5, 1848. He thus was able to introduce parliamentarism into Prussia without yielding to the principle of popular sovereignty; after all, the constitution was issued by virtue of *his* sovereign power, not the people's, and its authority was grounded therein. Thus, both conservatives and liberals had something to be cheer about.

The election campaign for the new constitutionally-estab-

---

[64]Barclay, 177ff.
[65]Schoeps, *Preussen: Geschichte eines Staats*, 201.
[66]Füßl, 156-157.

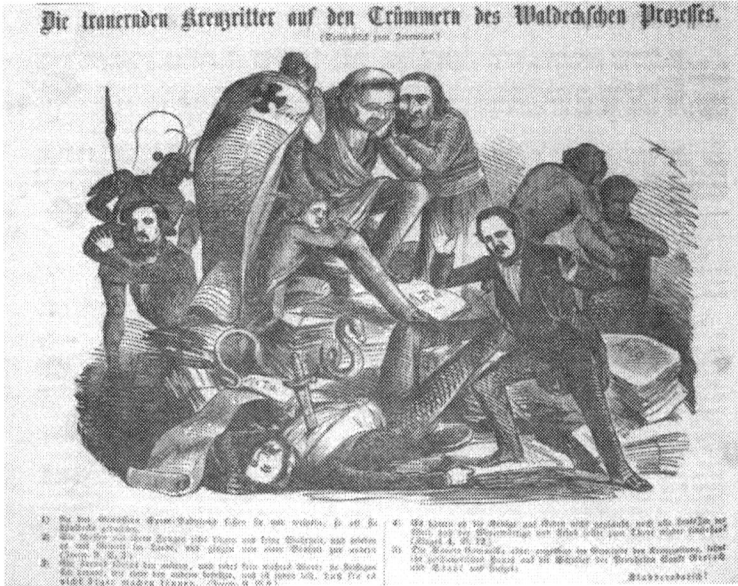

Kladderadatsch lamenting the dissolution of the Berlin Assembly. Stahl is pictured here as a crocodile-teared Jesuit.

lished assembly took place in January and February of 1849, and in it, Stahl played a key role in establishing a functioning conservative party. It was Stahl who had convinced conservatives that constitutionalism was not on its face antithetical to monarchy. For example, the *Kreuzzeitung* had been ambivalent about the concept of constitutional monarchy up until the time of Friedrich Wilhelm's patent. But with the election campaign, it showed itself a convert. Its articles breathed the spirit of Stahl's constitutional monarchy. The conservatives, with this unified perspective, were able to combine and carry on a successful campaign. For his part, Stahl stumped in favor of conservative candidates as well as for the party's agenda, allaying fears and doubts about the wisdom of the constitutional course. And having already garnered experience in the Bavarian parliament, he was viewed with great respect by the Prussians, who were new to this phenomenon of parliamentarism.

"Among conservatives of all stripes, Stahl was recognized as the unquestioned mastermind [Vordenker] of the party." Stahl ended up being elected to the first chamber. One of his fellow conservatives, an up-and-coming nobleman by the name of Otto von Bismarck, was elected to the second chamber.[67]

The next step was to build a party faction within the two houses of the parliament. To attain this end, a party platform needed to be written up; the task fell to Stahl. "It is difficult," writes Füßl, "to overestimate its fundamental importance."[68] The platform went beyond the generalities of the election campaign and outlined an agenda for future conservative politics. Such a political agenda, wrote Stahl, must "be the politics of both preservation and progress." It comprised seven main points:[69]

1. Allegiance to the "new order of the state," "the constitution as the legally chartered single order of the collective public condition," including "popular representation extending across all classes and its decisive participation in legislation," furthermore "the extension of individual freedom against preemptive police actions," and finally "the prospect of popular participation in government" in greater or lesser degree.

2. Allegiance to legality and respect for the ruling authorities; for conservatives could not recognize the Revolution as the principle behind the new order, even if it was its historical cause. "We much rather maintain the inviolability of the legal order, that it represent a limit

---

[67]Füßl, 162ff.; quotation, 173.
[68]Füßl, 182.
[69]The entire document is quoted verbatim in Füßl, 183ff.

to the arbitrary will of the people as hitherto it has to the arbitrary will of the prince." Therefore, due process of law is to be followed in all reforms, acquired rights are to be protected, freedom of expression is to be accorded all opinions whether popular or unpopular.

3. Allegiance to real, true monarchy; a monarchy which remains a personal relationship between sovereign and subject regardless of the extent of constitutional restrictions. "A personal relationship in the sense of the old Prussian slogan, with God for King and Fatherland!" Yes, a king within the constitution, but a king who must always have the final word in the form of a right of veto with regard to all legislation.

4. Allegiance to an articulated social order, a social order structured by classes. The conservative element in society is to be sought not exclusively in the upper classes but in all classes "through well-established institutions that unite them all, that bind the individual and his interests to the whole and to its order." To this end an upper house should be established in the parliament which serves as the primary guarantor of order and of the honor and respect due to the authorities.

5. A commitment to maintain a materially and ethically satisfying life for the working class, and to accept more far-reaching regulation and reorganization of working conditions as long as they truly and enduringly further this goal, without sacrificing due regard for all interests and without damaging the inalienable foundations of human society: property, inheritance, freedom of occupation.

6. A commitment to pan-German unification, but with the preservation of an appropriate level of self-govern-

ment for the individual states, especially Prussia, and
the maintenance of each people's particular way of life,
historical bonds, historical remembrances, and, for the
German union, popular representation only on a
strong monarchical basis.

7.   A commitment to equal political rights for all religious
confessions as an irrevocable grant; but at the same
time the protection by the state of the two previously
existing confessions (i.e., Lutheran and Reformed) or,
"in the case of the full separation of church and state,
the freedom of the church and the freedom of education."

The platform constituted a "milestone in the development
of a modern conservatism."[70] Interestingly, Stahl showed himself to be aware and forward-thinking in the area of economics
as well. "Years before the revolution [of March 1848 – RCA]
Stahl had integrated constitutional principles in his theory of
public law which other conservatives only recognized under
pressure from the events of the revolution; he acted in similar
manner with regard to the social welfare question, which in
1849 was not recognized by conservatives as a problem at
all."[71]

Even with such integrating guiding principles, however, the
conservatives were unable to attain the desired cohesion. In
part this was due to diverging opinions regarding the degree to
which constitutionalism and popular representation were to be
accepted within the monarchical framework. But a major con-
tributing factor was the whole problem of German unification,

---

[70]Füßl, 185.
[71]Füßl, 185.

still playing out in the National Assembly in Frankfurt, the fallout from which was having its impact even within the Prussian parliament. Events outside the Prussian assembly had usurped the spotlight.

5. The Attempt At Unification

All the while the Prussian parliamentary events had been unfolding, with the original assembly formed, then dissolved, and then a new assembly formed under the aegis of Friedrich Wilhelm's constitution by decree, the Frankfurt national assembly had been deliberating. The main focus of debate had been the drafting of a charter of "Basic Rights of the German People."[72] There was not much difficulty putting together a list of so-called negative rights: freedom of speech, of the press, of association; freedom from arbitrary arrest; civil equality, including restrictions on the power of the nobility, full equality to all religious groups including Jews, and the abolition of a religious test for public office.

Problems cropped up as the delegates labored to define the content of "positive" rights "in favor of political and social liberty."[73] For instance, what role should the church play in public life? Some argued that freedom of religion meant freedom *from* the church and the advancement of secular ideals by the state; others, that the church played a necessary role in maintaining popular religious belief, and that its role therein must not be infringed upon by the state. There was also the question of citizenship versus local autonomy and self-government. If all Germans were equally citizens, what rights had local communities to restrict membership, as they hitherto had done? Then there was the Economics Committee, charged with elaborating rights with regard to economic and industrial

---

[72]For this discussion, see Sheehan, *German History*, 684ff.
[73]Sheehan, 685.

issues. This committee received all manner of petitions requesting alleviation of privation and the creation of "social stability." A motion stemming from the committee establishing a right to work was rejected by the plenary assembly. Months of fruitless labor produced nothing of further use.

From the debate on basic rights, the assembly moved to the constitutional issue. There were two aspects involved. Firstly, the definition of sovereignty: who was sovereign, and how was this sovereignty expressed in institutions? Secondly, the definition of Germany: was everywhere where German was spoken to be considered Germany? That would include parts of Poland, Switzerland, and certainly Austria, which itself was bound in the Austro-Hungarian empire to many non-German-speaking nations.

The former question was answered by establishing a division of powers between a hereditary monarch and the popular assembly; the proposal establishing this arrangement narrowly passed, by a vote of 267 to 263. The latter question was essentially answered by Austria. The major issue here was how to include the Austro-Hungarian empire – only the German-speaking lands, or the entire empire? The assembly voted to allow only German-speaking lands to become members of the new *Reich*; the new Austrian government, formed in similar fashion to the Prussian post-revolutionary government by a sort of coup d'etat,[74] declared that it would only join the new *Reich* if all of the Austro-Hungarian empire were included. This ultimatum settled the question at least in its most important dimension – Austria had ruled itself out of a united Germany. The only alternative to a Habsburg as hereditary monarch was

---

[74]Schoeps, *Preussen: Geschichte eines Staates*, 205.

Friedrich Wilhelm IV of Prussia. The crown was offered him by a delegation from the assembly; he politely but resolutely declined. He wrote to his uncle, the King of Hanover, in much more decided tone: he could not accept such a "dog collar" chaining him to the Revolution.

As it happened, this was the high-water mark of the liberal movement. With Friedrich Wilhelm's reject-

Joseph von Radowitz

ion, the Frankfurt assembly had lost its legitimacy and its purpose. After some further fitful activity, it dissolved for good.

With this victory, Friedrich Wilhelm moved to establish his authority even more securely in Prussia. He dissolved the Berlin assembly and decreed a new electoral law, the infamous "Three-Class Suffrage" law that established a weighted system in favor of wealth and social status. The new assembly was decidedly more conservative, and certainly would work to adopt revisions to the provisional constitution (the one decreed by the king) that would be amenable to himself.

But the pan-German issue remained high on the agenda. And Friedrich Wilhelm was actively using it to further his own authority at home, especially among otherwise-recalcitrant liberals. In this he was supported and advised by Joseph von Radowitz, a Catholic of Hungarian descent who was pushing for Prussian-led German unification, even if it meant yielding significant ground to the forces of popular sovereignty.

Radowitz had conceived a plan which he felt would establish the monarchy on the firm foundation of enduring popular support. To this end he wished to harness the two main problems driving German politics of the day: the "German question" and the "social question."

> If Prussia could devise an effective, non-liberal strategy to deal with the problems of modern poverty, if it could succeed in becoming a 'social kingdom', then monarchy itself would emerge stronger, and Frederick William would attain that popularity for which he always yearned. And an imaginative response to the aspiration of the German national movement would, Radowitz believed, lead not only to an expansion of Prussian state power but also to the consolidation of monarchical institutions throughout Central Europe.[75]

Radowitz thus foreshadowed the method Bismarck successfully would apply to achieve German unification in the second *Reich*. The contradictions and conflicts in Prussian and broader German society would be overcome by appealing to a greater unity and an overarching state power capable of answering the desires of every constituent. But such an agenda required the full support of the monarch: Bismarck was able to receive that – Radowitz, in the end, was not. For a time, he was able to convince Friedrich Wilhelm of the advantageousness of his plan, and for that time it appeared that Prussia might well assume the leadership of a united, Austria-shorn Germany. But it was premature, not least because the conservatives of the *Kreuzzeitung*, and Stahl among them, were able to stave off the exchange of principled Christianity for power politics as the lodestar for Prussian foreign policy. "It is only 130 years later,"

---

[75]Barclay, 187.

wrote Schoeps in 1980, "but given the current mindset it is hardly conceivable anymore that a ruling class in government [could elevate] the victory of principle over the state interest and [glorify] the primacy of Idea over Power."[76]

Radowitz had once counted himself among the conservatives, but he experienced a change of heart after participating in the Frankfurt debates. After Friedrich Wilhelm refused the imperial crown, he had Radowitz come up with a modified plan whereby Prussia would lead in the formation of a closer union of German states excluding Austria, while Austria would be allowed to form a looser union with the resulting German federation. Radowitz's plan incorporated many of the elements of the original Frankfurt version.

The conservatives looked upon the new venture with horror. Not only was Radowitz willing to harness the Trojan horse of popular representation to the new federation, he was intent on ousting Austria. Both of these taken together would certainly spell the end of the monarchy, they felt, if not sooner then later.

Be that as it may: Stahl himself was enough of a realist to take a hard look at Radowitz's plan and judge it on its merits. More than that: Stahl likewise viewed German unification as a desirable goal; in fact, he believed passionately in it. But it, like church unification, could not be pursued at the expense of principle. It was precisely here that his path diverged from that of the Frankfurt liberals, and from Radowitz as well.

His passion both for German unification and for Prussian identity is evident from a speech he gave in the Berlin upper house concerning the Frankfurt assembly's election of Frie-

---

[76]Schoeps, *Das andere Preußen*, 89.

drich Wilhelm IV as emperor.

Gentlemen, when the German people arose more than thirty years ago, in order, in truly free and purely national elevation, to throw off foreign domination, Prussia led the way not only with weapons but also in German feeling and German essence. It was here that Körner, Schenkendorf and Arndt sang their German songs. Here Stein, Humboldt, Niebuhr founded a German politics, here Scharnhorst founded a German army the equal of which has not been seen since in Europe, and a hero of German character, Blücher, led that army to victory. The great mass movement of Europe against France at that time found its focus, its moral consecration and its explanation in Germany, and especially in Prussia. German enthusiasm here spread its wings, and everything that had a heart and a soul in Germany followed in its train. I was then a boy in southern Germany, yet untrained in weapons, but a beam of that enthusiasm fell upon my soul and that of the circle of youth of which I was a part, and I have preserved it as the best that I possessed. If I could here repay what I then received from here, I would sing a hymn to the Prussian people, what its fame was then, what its calling is now. Germany is not now in any less danger that it was in the years 1813 to 1815; may Prussia therefore again be the Prussia of 1813 and 1814 and 1815, may it be the sword of Germany through its armed forces, may it be the example of Germany through its political institutions and the spirit that pervades them. Therefore… allow us to recommend a policy to our government which in equal measure pursues the unity of Germany, the power of Prussia and the preservation of the rights of all princes and all German clans [Stämme]. Thereby will the Holy Empire of the German Nation once again arise; because it is the venerable character of that Empire, that it regard and comport itself as a divine protectorate [Schirmherrschaft], "preserving each in his own" (stenographer's note: Bravo).[77]

---

[77]Stahl, *Siebzehn parlamentarische Reden*, 131-132.

"Reaction on the Tree of Liberty": *Kladderadatsch* caricatures the conservatives' opposition to the Union bill of rights; Stahl is once again portrayed as a Jesuit.

For unification to go forward, Stahl argued that three conditions be met:[78] that Prussia must be accorded its independence within the framework of a federal union and a central government, i.e., that Prussia and the other large German states be allowed to keep their own governments; next, that the princes of Germany should be maintained in their authority, and that sovereignty should be vested in them and not the people per se; thirdly, that Prussia should become the standing federal head – Austria was unsuited for this task, its empire extending to non-German peoples. Austria could then join in a looser union with the German federation as a whole. He thus cautiously signed on to Radowitz's project, albeit stipulating significant changes away from popular sovereignty and towards monarchy.

Stahl took seriously the modified version now put forward by Radowitz and the Prussian government because it proceeded under the auspices of the kings of Prussia, Hanover, and Saxony: the so-called *Dreikönigsbündnis*, the "Three-King's Alliance." As a result, it was much more "prince-friendly." He argued in favor of further union under Prussian leadership in a series of articles published in the *Kreuzzeitung* in May 1849.

This was a courageous move, given that it spelled isolation; Stahl could count on support neither from the liberals nor from the conservatives. Most conservatives were consciously opposed to the whole project, precisely because they feared the forces of revolution it might further unleash, and because of the alienation it could bring about with Austria, that anchor of the monarchical principle. But Stahl was unwilling to write off the project ahead of time. He felt that German unification under Prussian leadership would provide the best guarantee for

---

[78]Füßl, 199.

Protestantism and monarchy. Austria had embarked on a reactionary course that was grounded in the unworkable desire to turn back the clock; mere adherence to it and similarly autocratic Russia would not stave off the forces of popular participation forever.

Approaching the issue on its merits, Stahl found much of value in the new proposal. But he also subjected it to thoroughgoing critique, which because it took the project seriously was much more effective than simple negativism. For his part, Friedrich Wilhelm recognized in Stahl someone who was more than a knee-jerk reactionary, and therefore paid special attention to him and his followers.[79]

Stahl found the new version much improved on the Frankfurt constitution. Its electoral law was more restricted, with the lower house of the diet elected according to the Prussian three-class arrangement. Nevertheless, he did criticize its blatant imitation of the United States Congress. In Stahl's view, the US could not serve as a model for Germany, because it was a republic composed of republics, while Germany was a nation of monarchies. Stahl would have a diet composed of a lower house chosen by the assemblies of the various constituent states, and an upper house composed of representatives of the ruling princes.[80]

One great improvement in Stahl's view was the addition of a College of Princes [*Fürstenkollegium*], a separate house alongside the diet which together with it and the federal head would perform the legislative function. Stahl furthermore was satisfied with the way in which the new constitutional proposal reserved power to the constituent states in much greater de-

---

[79]Füßl, 215.
[80]Füßl, 212.

gree than did the Frankfurt version.[81]

One of the areas of which Stahl was most critical was that of a declaration of fundamental rights. He was not opposed in principle to such declarations as long as they were grounded in historic growth and social reality. He was critical of the extensive catalog of rights included in the Frankfurt constitution because it "exceeded the measure of what is practical and necessary."[82] In Stahl's view, rights are historically acquired liberties, but they needed to be offset by public security: and for this reason such rights needed first and foremost to guarantee the Christian foundations of the state. "Stahl believed that civil society in its essential structures would be dissolved by the elaborate catalog of basic rights issued by the Frankfurt parliament. Under these he included the Christian faith, its implementation in the schools and in Christian marriage, the unrestricted disposition of property, and the maintenance of the death penalty as security against violence."[83] The new proposal was much improved in that it provided guidelines to the constituent states rather than an obligatory list; it also rejected the notion of religious equality, implicitly recognizing Christianity as the state religion.[84]

Opposition from both left and right put Prussia's Union project on shaky ground. The initial 26 states that had agreed to join it dwindled over time to a group of smaller states in northern and central Germany. There was external pressure from Austria and skepticism from the southern and western, predominantly Catholic, German states; and there was internal

---

[81]Füßl, 211-212.
[82]Quoted in Füßl, 213.
[83]Füßl, 214.
[84]*Ibid.*

pressure, both from democrats upset with the restricted suffrage law and from the aforementioned conservatives. Nevertheless, the remaining participants agreed to go forward with
the plan, in January 1850 conducting elections to a Union parliament to be convened in Erfurt the following March.

As in 1849, the conservatives pulled together to fight the
campaign. Rather than write off the government-sponsored
Union project, they campaigned in favor of amending the constitution as then proposed. Following Stahl's recommenda-
tions, the primary focus of amendment was the section on basic rights. The conservatives of Stahl's orientation laid special
emphasis on the Christian foundation of the state, criticizing
the catalog of rights on this basis. This pitted the conservatives
against the Prussian government and Friedrich Wilhelm, who,
following Radowitz, insisted on the acceptance of the constitution as proposed.

Elections in the Union states took place on January 30, and
resulted in a resounding success for the conservatives, mainly
because democrats and many liberals were opposed to the plan
from the start. Stahl was elected and became the head of the
so-called Schlehdorn fraction. As such, he became the leading
figure among the conservatives; none could match his talents
either in terms of political acumen or constitutional law. "Valued by the king and the government as negotiating partner,
accepted by the Camarilla and recognized by like-minded persons as the leader of the party since the end of 1848, Stahl now
became the central figure in Prussian conservatism. As he did
in the Prussian upper house, Stahl assumed the leadership of
the right wing in the People's House [*Volkshaus*] in Erfurt,
there experiencing incontestably his greatest parliamentary suc-

cess."[85]

During this time Stahl's position both in terms of principle and within the constellation of forces in Prussian politics bore its most significant fruit. The king and the government were pushing for the assembly to ratify the proposed constitution "en bloc," as a whole, as were the so-called "Gothaer" liberals, holdovers from the Frankfurt assembly. The conservatives, on the other hand, were dead set against this, as they wished to strengthen the Christian, monarchical, and Prussian positions within it, and this by means of amendments prior to ratification.

To win the conservatives over, Friedrich Wilhelm held an audience at his estate in Charlottenberg, inviting conservative leaders such as Ludwig von Gerlach, a vociferous opponent, and Otto von Bismarck (who however was out of town at the time), along with Stahl. Friedrich Wilhelm impressed upon them the need to support the government, as an expression of loyalty to the king. He held out positions in government as an enticement, and warned of a complete break in case they opposed him, which for them would constitute a political death sentence. They must go along with the government's position regarding ratification "en bloc;" if this was not done, two-thirds of the participating governments would withdraw from the process.[86]

Stahl answered that in terms of constitutional law the proposed constitution would nullify Prussia's influence in the Union and make the Union government, and in particular the Union's proposed supreme court, supreme in Prussian internal

---

[85]Füßl, 238.

[86]The account of this audience recounted in these paragraphs is taken from Füßl, 231ff.

affairs. And after ratification, Prussia could not withdraw from the Union as the king liked to think, if things did not go Prussia's way, without violating basic principles of justice. Ratification was binding. Stahl emphasized that the conservatives were not opposed to the government's goal but only to ways of achieving it; the approach of the parliamentary party would smooth the way for achieving the kind of constitutional revision both it and the government wanted.

The meeting ended with the king upset at Stahl's insistence that ratification would be binding on Prussia, as he fancied things otherwise; but the olive branch Stahl offered in terms of cooperation with the government was not overlooked. Stahl would remain an important figure in the king's efforts to create the Union. In fact, the king thereafter would compel Radowitz to adopt Stahl's agenda for amending the constitution.

The Erfurt assembly opened for business some days after this audience, on March 20. The lower house, to which Stahl had been elected, was presided over by Radowitz. Because of the king's change of heart, Radowitz was forced to declare against his own position of "en bloc" ratification and in favor of piecemeal amendment. In doing so, he gained the support of Stahl's fraction and the conservatives, but alienated the liberals.

In his maiden speech in the People's House, delivered on 12 April 1849, Stahl lent support to the Prussian government's position. The effect of his speech was electrifying. Two liberal members could not but admit otherwise.

> Herr Stahl handled the word with a mastery the likes of which we did not even hear in the Paulskirche [i.e., the Frankfurt assembly – RCA]. The abundance of his thoughts, the boldness of his turns, the beauty of his examples, affected the assembly with an

indescribable magic, which was completely amazed by the brilliant dialectic form which with wonderful gracefulness adapted on the spur of the moment a multifarious material drawn largely from the words of the previous speaker. Herr Stahl's speech was finished like a work of art, without shortcoming, in terms of political achievement a masterpiece of astuteness.[87]

It was in this speech that Stahl uttered his memorable aphorism, "Authority, Not Majority," which forms both the title of this book and the clearest statement of his philosophy.[88]

Stahl subjected the proposal to a detailed examination in an extended discussion, *Die deutsche Reichsverfassung*. One of the major areas of his critique concerned the proposed supreme court.[89] The constitution provided for the establishment of a supreme court with ultimate sovereignty: it "grants a sort of *sovereign position* to the Imperial Court as a power over all elements of the Empire, so that in the last analysis the entire imperial constitution receives its interpretation and application, and thus the putting right of its relations, through its sentence."[90] This power, Stahl argued, focused on three areas. Firstly, the court had power to decide the boundaries of jurisdiction between the central government and the individual state governments. Secondly, the court could decide cases between the central government and individual citizens with regard to the violation of individual rights. Thirdly, it had the power to decide constitutional conflicts between state administrations and state assemblies. Stahl considered this arrangement to be dangerous and unacceptable, especially in a situa-

---

[87]Quoted in Füßl, 245.

[88]This speech is referenced more fully below, p. 115 ff.

[89]Füßl, 220ff.

[90]Stahl, *Die deutsche Reichsverfassung*, 51.

tion, such as the present, where the constitutional life of the
nation is uncertain and has to be built up. "In such constitutions one must leave the actual settlement to the parties who,
none being certain of the outcome, agree in fairness, and to the
influences of life with its undeniable needs, and to the sentiment of the core of the population; one should not submit it
to the precise treatment of the judge."[91] Against this, Stahl argued in favor of an organic approach in which differences between constitutional members are settled through practical
agreement and pragmatic concern for what works, rather than
through judicial decree. His example: the Protestant church in
the 17th century, which had no supreme court to decide
differences of doctrine, but which nevertheless saw these
differences ironed out through a process of historical development.[92]

In Erfurt as earlier in Berlin, Stahl's principled yet practical
position provided the conservatives with an alternative to sliding off into pointless and irrelevant reaction. As he had done
with constitutional monarchy, Stahl was able to convince his
party members of the necessity of a tempered policy toward
unification.[93] Together with the Prussian government, they
solidified a conservative position that disentangled the movement for national unity from revolutionary popular sovereignty.

Initially the liberals got their way, voting in favor of "en
bloc" ratification. Nevertheless, the assembly then had to
amend the constitution in accordance with the wishes of the
Prussian government. The result was submitted by the Union

---

[91]Stahl, *Die deutsche Reichsverfassung*, 56.
[92]Füßl, 222.
[93]Füßl, 250.

executive to the member states for approval. This was to be considered in a Congress of Princes.

Stahl's work in the People's House had thus borne its merited fruit. The constitution was cast in the image he had presented, Radowitz and the Prussian government had argued for it, and the assembly had accepted it. No wonder that the conservatives in the assembly held a dinner party in his honor shortly before adjournment. Ludwig von Gerlach, colleague and critic, raised a toast to him, memorializing the phrase he had uttered on the spur of the moment on the floor of Parliament: "Authority, not majority."[94]

Meanwhile, Austria's opposition to the Union project was gaining momentum. Austria formed its own League of Four Kings, including Bavaria, Württemberg, and Saxony, to rival Prussia's Union project. It insisted that it must not be left out of any such project, and could not accept the Prussian proposal of a narrower union without Austria and a broader union with it. The conservatives of the *Kreuzzeitung* and the Camarilla, which still exerted great influence on Friedrich Wilhelm and his government, increasingly distanced themselves from Radowitz and the Union project, becoming ever more vehement in their opposition as Austria became more antagonistic.

What was Stahl's position during this period of escalating tension? One the one hand, Radowitz was pushing for confrontation and military conflict if need be; on the other, the *Kreuzzeitung* and the Camarilla were pulling out all the stops to divert the government from its collision course with Austria, even if that meant abandoning the unification project altogether. Friedrich Wilhelm hesitated between the two courses.

---

[94]Füßl, 252-253. See 66 above, 115 below.

Aus Berlin.

Aber bester Professor, wie kommen Sie denn auf diesen Ball, Sie, der Repräsentant des christlichen Staates?! Ich wollte mir nur einmal wieder den jüdischen Staat ansehen.

"But my dear Professor, how do you come to the ball, you, the representative of the *Christian state?* – I wished to look upon the *Jewish state* once more." *Kladderadatsch* caricaturing Stahl's political philosophy.

Stahl abstained altogether from public pronouncements on the matter.[95] His view was neither that of the other conservatives nor of the unionists. Here again, his attempt to steer clear

---

[95]Füßl, 262f.

of both Scylla and Charybdis was in evidence. He viewed Austria with a jaundiced eye as pursuing bureaucratic absolutism and the destruction of valid constitutional liberties. Of the three members of the Holy Alliance of 1815, only Prussia was making the attempt to move into the modern age by way of constitutional government. In a prescient passage he described both the outcome of immediate conflict with Austria (which in the event occurred just as he foresaw) and the ultimate result of a rupture between Prussia and Austria – the undoing of Christian monarchy in Germany:

> It is possible that when things come to a head, Prussia will bow to superior forces, since Russia will take Austria's side. That will however spell the end of all thrones, at any rate it will be the ruin of the holy principles of the German condition. Austria, which combines the most backward profession of Catholicism with despotic power, which offered up its most deserving general to revolutionary ministers, will not maintain them. Prussia is the representative of the Protestant principle in Germany and therefore also of true German civilization. The smaller states could through their support for Austria contribute thereto to destroying or weakening this refuge, but they will not be capable of toppling each other from the throne [nicht imstande sein einander zu schassen], they will, against the Fatherland, precipitate their decline in the Austrian or finally the Russian manner, against which they cannot stand.[96]

In the event, the conservatives gained the day. Prussian and Austrian troops faced each other down in Hesse and even exchanged a few shots before Prussia extended the olive branch. Friedrich Wilhelm and minister–president Brandenburg finally decided to let Radowitz go and be reconciled with Austria. The

---

[96]Stahl to Hassenpflug, in Koglin, 361-362.

price was the abandonment of Prussia-led unification and a return to the days of the Austrian-led German Confederation.

Thus dawned what the liberals came to refer to as "the Years of Reaction," in which the conservatives supposedly ruled the roost. But what really had been accomplished was the fracturing of the Holy Alliance by the states the conservatives had looked to for stability and the maintenance of legitimism in the face of the threat of revolution. As Stahl predicted, Austria's triumph was a Pyrrhic victory which ultimately led to the defeat of Christian monarchy in Europe, as would become evident during the course of the 1850s. Likewise, it was the time when Stahl's agenda in both church and state started to be abandoned by his conservative friends in Prussia. The day of reckoning was nearing for Prussia, and for Germany.

6. Rearguard Action

Concurrent with the Erfurt national assembly, the Prussian assembly reconvened in Berlin to deliberate over further revisions to the provisional Prussian constitution, which had been promulgated by Friedrich Wilhelm at the end of 1848. As was the case with the Erfurt assembly, Stahl led the conservative fraction in the upper house of the Berlin assembly. The "Stahl fraction" exercised an influence belying its small size. This influence was gained through Stahl's principled yet practical approach, which the king valued and which positioned Stahl as a mediator between fractions in Parliament and between the parliament itself and the Prussian government.

Three issues were in the forefront of the debate, which constituted the dividing line between liberal and conservative: the right of the parliament to review taxes; the question of ministerial accountability to the parliament; and the shape of the upper house. All of these constituted hot-button issues, the solution of which was facilitated by Stahl's incisive analysis and prescriptions.

The liberals in the assembly held fast to the notion that the parliament must be accorded the right periodically to review and either renew or refuse existing tax revenues. Their view of the constitution was that it was the monarchy that needed controlling, and the assembly had to have the tools available to exercise that control; and the most effective tool to that end was that provided by purse strings.

They viewed this power as balancing the scales between assembly and monarchy; Stahl, for his part, recognized in this power the decisive tilting of the scales in favor of Parliament.

As he warned, it was not constitutional monarchy which would be established by such a provision, but democracy itself. The example of the English lower house was telling. There, the House of Commons had gained the power of the purse, and with this power had inexorably gained control of the government, to the point that the king no longer exercised any meaningful authority. The same would happen in Prussia if this revision was accepted.

Now, in England this power is in the hands of a responsible aristocracy, but in Prussia, in whose hands would this power fall? In a speech to the assembly, Stahl posed the question: "But I ask, gentlemen, do we have an English popular representation, that we can be satisfied with a king on the English model? What do have for representation anyway? We don't even know ourselves" (stenographer's note: hilarity).[97] The English model was a unique outgrowth of historical circumstances and could not simply be grafted into German conditions.

As neither liberal nor conservative wished to establish a democracy per se, Stahl's advice was heeded. Things went differently regarding the question of ministerial responsibility, which naturally was a subject of heated dispute. Were the ministers in government responsible to the king, who appointed and dismissed them, or were they also accountable to the assembly, which could subject them to a vote of no confidence? Obviously, for Stahl and his fellow conservatives ministerial accountability to the assembly was out of the question, as it would undermine the monarchical element of constitutional monarchy.

This issue did not move to the center of political interest in

---

[97]Stahl, *Siebzehn parliamentarische Reden*, 13.

Prussia until the issues surrounding the conflict with Austria were resolved at the end of 1850. Early in 1851, Stahl was among those chosen by the upper house to form a commission to deliberate over the government's proposed legislation. In fact, he was chosen as the commission's spokesman.

The commission's – Stahl's – proposal integrated elements of the liberals' conception with Stahl's basic monarchical orientation. It would simplify the procedure for calling a minister to account, thus incorporating one of the liberals' proposals, but would make such a call contingent on approval by both houses. The assembly therefore would be allowed to call ministers to account; but on the other hand, the proposal stipulated that such a call could not carry over into a new parliamentary session. The king therefore by dissolving the assembly and calling for new elections could nullify the procedure.

The government would not even go along with this watered-down version. And without the government's support, the proposal was doomed to failure. In the end, no provision to implement ministerial accountability was ever adopted. The king could "hire and fire" as he wished, but even in this case there was no procedure for establishing how exactly a minister *as minister* was responsible for his actions. What this situation led to was ministerial autonomy, as the king was loath to dismiss ministers for fear of getting something worse in return. And this ministerial autonomy in turn fed the tendency toward the bureaucratization of the state, one of the nefarious trends of the 1850s.

Stahl's viewpoint fared better in the question of the composition of the upper house. Friedrich Wilhelm was dead set on transforming that house from the electoral basis upon which it

Friedrich Wilhelm IV (1847)

was set in the provisional constitution into one modeled on the British House of Lords, where he himself would choose its members.

Stahl along with his conservative cohorts fought the king's intention tooth and nail. Stahl argued that such an upper house, while suited to conditions in Great Britain, was totally unsuited to the situation in Prussia, where a high nobility was relatively lacking. Stahl's upper house would represent the "power" and "esteem" of individuals, groups, or institutions as they actually existed in Prussia. It would include adult princes of the blood, heads of households who had counted among the estates of the Old Reich; landowners possessing an income greater than 8000 thalers, chosen by the king; the largest landowners from each province; the largest industrialists and merchants from each province; the eight superintendents of the Protestant church and the eight Catholic bishops; representatives from the leading cities of each province; and representatives from each university. It was a complicated system, combining criteria of status and election.[98] One thing Stahl did not want was for the upper house to become a tool of the government, which is why he wished to anchor its criteria for selection firmly in the constitution rather than leave selection up to the king. His motivation was

---

[98]Füßl, 302.

the same as in the case of his proposal regarding ministerial accountability: "His measures for safeguarding against an overweening government ministry is such a prominent characteristic of Stahl's practical-political demands that they must expressly be seen in this context."[99] Stahl and his conservative counterparts feared burgeoning bureaucracy just as they feared burgeoning democracy.

For his part, Friedrich Wilhelm would not be diverted from his course. "In a widely circulated memorandum of 19 January 1852, the monarch declared, '*I demand to be the one and only organizer of the First Chamber*', an arrangement which he described as essential for the '*honour, prestige, and future of the Prussian crown*'."[100] Stahl viewed the king's proposal in an entirely different light. Far from helping to maintain the crown, such an upper house would be sidelined because unrepresentative, and the true center of gravity of Prussian politics would shift to the lower house. Stahl wanted the upper house to be a support for monarchy but also to be independent, a voice in its own right not only for monarchy but for the common interest.

Stahl laid out his argument in a celebrated speech delivered in the upper house on March 5, 1852, which has been characterized as "a turning point in Prussian conservatism" and which was viewed by a contemporary as "arguably his best speech, in any case his most brilliant."[101] In it he particularly argued for the importance of the Junkers, the landed gentry which formed the backbone of monarchical and Lutheran, "throne and altar" sentiment.[102]

---

[99]Füßl, 304.

[100]Barclay, 247.

[101]Füßl, 332.

[102]The full text of this speech is contained in Stahl's *Siebzehn*

Stahl was skeptical of the king's intention politically to replace this class in the upper house with a "high nobility" on
the model of the English House of Lords. The English Lords
had pedigrees of hundreds of years, were originally barons at
the side of William the Conqueror, were never created ex nihi-
lo by a wave of the king's hand. Besides, the Lords as they
originally existed are no longer encountered anywhere in Europe. "Those great Lords with their vassals and undervassals,
with their tenants and undertenants, which at the head of a
whole entire dependent population formed an equal significant
power over against other whole populations, and therefore
could be established as a House over against the other Houses,
where are such still to be found?"[103] Nowadays the high nobility does not represent anything more than its own family. If a
counterweight is to be found to the lower house, it must be the
entire landed aristocracy taken together, not a few houses set
apart. The influence of the English House of Lords was ebb-
ing, precisely for this reason.

The king, Stahl continued, wanted to reserve the upper
house for a "high nobility" and consign the "low nobility," the
Junkers, to the lower house. "That it is not the intention to
eliminate the landed aristocracy... but only for it to take its
place in the lower house, appears to me to be pure fiction, in
that it never had a place in the lower house; for the possessors
of manorial estates to compete for votes with proletarians cannot be called representation of the landed aristocracy" (stenographer's note: restlessness, calls of Yes! Yes!).[104]

It was argued that a "high nobility" would not have its own

parliamentarische Reden, 70-85.

[103]Stahl, *Siebzehn parliamentarische Reden*, 78.
[104]Stahl, *Siebzehn parliamentarische Reden*, 77-78.

interests in mind but would represent the common interest.

> Those grands Seigneurs who, as it is hoped, under threatening conditions will, like the Duke of Noailles, lay their rights on the altar of the Fatherland, appear to me in no way to be a more valuable element than the small landed Junker who defends not only his own rights but the rights of his King to the last drop of blood. If the gentry really contains a reactionary element, it actually argues in its favor. We are in need of the strongest reactionary forces until we have entirely removed the poison of the Revolution that circulates in the vitals of the nation" (stenographer's note: Bravo! from the right).[105]

In pre-March 1848 Prussia, the landed aristocracy served as the main element of representation. As such,

> the question is not the establishment of an aristocracy but the maintenance of a real, existing aristocracy. The Prussian aristocracy in particular was the nation's representative until 1848.... The consequence of [this proposal] is that it entirely lose its position as representative of the nation, which would spell the elimination of its political existence. Is it advisable to eliminate this last solid core from former times? Have contemporary times anywhere laid such fixed, unshakeable foundations? Have we all... demonstrated ourselves so creative in the founding of new institutions that we can allow ourselves to sacrifice the inheritance of a richer and more creative past?[106]

The landed aristocracy no longer occupies the preeminent position in the nation, that is true. Trade and industry, an enlightened bureaucracy, now occupy their own positions of power. But for this reason to remove political power from the

---

[105]Stahl, *Siebzehn parliamentarische Reden*, 78-79.
[106]Stahl, *Siebzehn parliamentarische Reden*, 79-80.

landed aristocracy would be the unwisest thing to which a leg-
islator could aspire.

> That ancient element, the landed aristocracy, represents in the
> main, although happily not exclusively, the former way of thinking
> of this country. It has set its face to the past in full reverence for
> the honors, the morals, the rights of ancient times, and when one
> nevertheless makes the objection that in its pettiness, its tenacity,
> its narrow-mindedness it is restricting the progress and the foun-
> dation of the greatness of Prussia, I believe I can retort in full
> measure. Because the elements of modern times, with their faces
> to the future, are predominantly the purveyors of the destructive
> doctrines of the present. Or does one believe that the scientific
> intelligence of the bureaucracy has kept itself pure from the de-
> structive tendencies – is it perchance any different here than in
> France, Westphalia, Bavaria, anywhere in Europe, anytime at all?
> Does anyone believe that the undeniably justified needs of the
> times will be fulfilled in some other way here than according to
> the general ruling principles of the Revolution? The great political
> value of the landed aristocracy is that it has been anything but
> receptive to these new doctrines or principles, whether due to self-
> interest or patriotism, pettiness or profundity.[107]

An independent upper house is an indispensable element of
Prussian politics and an indispensable support of the crown,
and its ability to support the crown is grounded precisely in its
independence. And the heart of an independent upper house is
that venerable Junker class. The alternative to it was the institutions of the Revolution and rule by bureaucracy.

Was Stahl, as his detractors claimed, simply an apologist of
this class? "I am not a supporter of the crown for the sake of
the aristocracy, I am a supporter of the aristocracy for the sake

---

[107]Stahl, *Siebzehn parliamentarische Reden*, 81.

of the crown" (stenographer's note: Bravo! from the right).[108]
Furthermore, Stahl was himself no aristocrat and bound by no
personal interest to that class. "Neither personal interest nor
social relations attach me to the aristocracy, I am only politically attached to the right wing of this House, in which the
aristocracy forms a significant element. It is the army in which
until now I have served" (stenographer's note: Bravo!).[109]

Eventually Friedrich Wilhelm was forced to compromise,
and he compromised in the direction of Stahl's proposal.[110] In
1854 a new House of Lords was established, a House based
not on elections but on the king's appointment – appoint-
ments, however, which could only be made from among restricted groups in accordance with Stahl's criteria. Such a compromise typified Stahl's approach to politics, one of flexibility
yet not losing sight of the underlying principle.

The Christian confession was the main bond of political
conservatives. "The shared religious life formed a strong connection. They [the conservatives – RCA] were together in discussion circles concerning religious themes, encountered each
other in prayer groups, together attended Sunday services at
the Church of St. Matthew."[111] One critic did not think much
of Stahl's circle: "This guy [diesen Kopf] has a monstrous
swarm of narrow-minded people hanging around him who
view *this journal* [i.e., the *Kreuzzeitung* – RCA] *as an extension of the
Bible for politics*, and on top of that a herd of political women
and young ladies, making it a wasps' nest that has to be

---

[108]Stahl, *Siebzehn parliamentarische Reden*, 83-84.
[109]Stahl, *Siebzehn parliamentarische Reden*, 84.
[110]Barclay, 249.
[111]Nabrings, 147.

eliminated."[112]

It was this Christianity in its public dimension which was threatened by another article in the provisional constitution, which on the one hand guaranteed freedom of religion but on the other eliminated the specific Christian character of Prussia's political institutions. Stahl argued against the provisional constitution in a speech to the upper house delivered in 1849, on "The Separation of Church and State."[113]

Stahl spoke in favor of a revision to the constitution to add the following statement: "Christianity remains authoritative for all public institutions standing in connection with religion. The Protestant and the Roman Catholic church retain their public-national standing in the state."[114] Stahl listed the immediate consequences of this clause: only Christian holidays would hold as general national holidays; the specifically Christian form of the oath would be maintained, along with an optional general oath; the Christian church would be empowered publically to perform marriages, along with civil marriages for those so wishing; chairs of theology of both recognized Christian churches, as against any other churches, would be maintained at all state universities; public schools would retain their Christian character. Furthermore, clergymen would become recognized as public servants, both recognized churches would have access to political rights and statuses not available to other religious communities, such as the public legitimation of their acts and their representation in both houses of the assembly, and both churches would exercise joint oversight over public education. "Hereby we desire that the Prussian nation

---

[112]Nabrings, 148.
[113]Stahl, *Siebzehn parliamentarische Reden*, 95-107.
[114]Stahl, *Siebzehn parliamentarische Reden*, 97.

henceforth in its entirety declare for Christianity, not as the religion of the majority but as the religion of the truth."[115]

What then of freedom of religion? Did not such a public, national confession obviate the commitment to such freedom, did it not violate conscience? Not at all:

> With all of this, religious freedom is not infringed; it may continue to exist in the widest possible degree, even in hyperextension, as it did in Article 11 as it originally stood. Regardless of one's religious opinion, his political rights will be preserved – only this, that the public institutions will not have to conform to his religious opinion; public institutions must be determined by the moral conviction of the nation in its unity, and the center of this moral conviction is its religious belief; this seems to me the harmonious balance between the claims of individual freedom and rights (even in their most exaggerated forms) on the one hand and on the other hand that which is and must remain the task of the state, the bond of national unity.[116]

The Christian character of the state therefore could and should coexist with free participation in government for adherents of all religious faiths – an echo of T.S. Eliot's *The Idea of a Christian Society*.

The proposed separation of church and state will lead to the denial of the Christian religion and its replacement either by the religion of reason or no religion at all. As in the days of Roman polytheism, the only religion that will not be tolerated will be the Christian. And anti-Christian sentiment, in turn, is the breeding ground of socialism: "the republican-socialist propaganda that in recent years through underground activity spread its net across all of Europe and with a jerk toppled

---

[115]Stahl, *Siebzehn parliamentarische Reden*, 98.
[116]Stahl, *Siebzehn parliamentarische Reden*, 99.

thrones had as its center the abolition of Christianity, the abolition of religion... ." It is no longer the mild, rational religion of
humanity propagated among cultured circles during the Enlightenment that now stands over against Christianity, but
atheism and pantheism and fanatical irreligiosity. "It is no longer amiable flippancy that stands over against strict Christian
morality, but the determined savagery of destruction, of dissolution and overthrow. Christian faith in God and the pronounced hatred of God, these are the two powers which now
move the life of the peoples in their deepest foundations."
There is no neutrality here; every inch of ground not held by
the Christian faith will be conquered by this implacable enemy.[117]

The advocates of the separation of church and state use the
example of the United States as an argument in their favor. But
the United States is in no way as secular as they think. It holds
to strict Sunday observance; the daily sessions of Congress are
opened with prayer by a Christian clergyman. There the situation is different: from the beginning, Christianity has permeated public life; in America, "unbeliever" is an insult the way
"pietist" is in Germany. "If we exchange situations, I would
happily accede to such a separation." Public life there is based
on entirely different elements: since the founding of the colo-
nies it has been based on the principle of voluntarism. Churches and schools, all public interests, are there furnished by local
communities and associations – "the state is scarcely encountered." Here as in France, on the other hand, public life rests
on the authority of the state and on the provision of the state.
If in America the state becomes de-Christianized, public life
can remain intact; here, public life and public education would

---

[117]Stahl, *Siebzehn parliamentarische Reden*, 103.

become de-Christianized.[118]

Another objection to public Christianity is that it supposedly hinders free political development. If that is the case, then why have England and North America come to an adequate condition of political freedom, and the French not? One factor is crucial: in England and America, the movement for liberty from the beginning was filled with the Christian faith, while in France it was directed against that faith. The freedom of England and America is permeated with the breath of the Puritans, that of France is permeated with the breath of the Encyclopedists [i.e., Enlightenment philosophers – RCA] and the Jacobins.

> Would that we would apply that to ourselves! As long as that breath of Christian faith does not vivifyingly go out over our Fatherland, our political efforts will remain fruitless. We can convene as many national assemblies from the nation's elite, from the most upright men, as we like…. The glue of our [German] states hitherto has been obedience to the government for God's sake, either from consciousness or habit. What will take its place? Something like the rational education of the people regarding the distinction between constitutional monarchy and democratic monarchy, the distinction between monarchy without an absolute veto and monarchy with an absolute veto, together with an absolute right to refuse taxes? Let us assume that the people of the nation understand these distinctions more easily than I do with my difficulty in understanding. I still fear that this glue would not hold for very long.[119]

Even the so-called "social question," the question of wealth and poverty, will find no other solution than in principles of

---

[118]Stahl, *Siebzehn parliamentarische Reden*, 104.
[119]Stahl, *Siebzehn parliamentarische Reden*, 105-106.

basic Christian virtue. Here Stahl echoes Thomas Chalmers:[120]

> The material need of the people and the resulting discontent, this great danger to the state order, is to be solved by mere national-economic measures apart from the motive of industriousness, thrift, frugal habits, an ordered family life? And are these motives to be gained without a living faith in the Christian revelation? The disruption of marriages is a chief cause of poverty, and is the most certain means of combating this to be introduction of civil marriages?[121]

We cannot allow ourselves to be deceived, Stahl warns; the Revolution is overcome but it is not annihilated. "We are living on a volcano, and if it does not now erupt, it still continues to smolder and we know not what period of respite we still have." What means do we have to close up this volcano? Some will say free-thinking concessions. But these haven't helped where they have been introduced, but have only made matters worse. Others will say energetic reaction. But that was what Metternich tried, and did that work? Now we have those who say that it will be accomplished by attaining national unity – but France has achieved that, and the crater of Revolution is still gaping there. "No! This damage lies deeper and can only be healed from the inside. Concessions, reaction and the satisfaction of longings for German unity are all good in their place, but they will not shut down the Revolution. Only Christianity, the Christian state and the Christian school will shut down the Revolution in Europe (stenographer's note: Bravo!

---

[120]One of Chalmers' works, on the care of the poor, was translated into German by another member of the Prussian conservative brain trust, Otto von Gerlach.

[121]Stahl, *Siebzehn parliamentarische Reden*, 106.

from the right).[122]

In the end, the upper and lower houses adopted the following provision, which became Article 14 of the constitution: "The Christian religion is laid at the foundation of those institutions in the state which stand in connection to the exercise of religion, notwithstanding the freedom of religion guaranteed in Article 12."[123] Stahl et al.'s original proposal therefore was essentially adopted (cf. pg. 82 above).

Nevertheless, Stahl's warnings proved to be prophetic. Despite this clause in the constitution, the Prussian state would soon drift from its moorings in Christianity. But Stahl would not give up without a fight or a proper witness. That is the subject of the following chapter.

---

[122]Stahl, *Siebzehn parliamentarische Reden,* 106-107.
[123]Stahl, *Siebzehn parliamentarische Reden,* 95.

7. The End of an Era

Stahl was busy with more than just politics during the "Period of Reaction" in the 1850s. The reader will recall that Friedrich Wilhelm, following Stahl's advice, in 1848 established a supreme consistory to oversee ecclesiastical affairs. This consistory did not get down to business until the fallout of the March revolution had settled. In 1850 it got down to business, with oversight over matters of church discipline, synodal affairs, and church doctrine and liturgy. Friedrich Wilhelm appointed Stahl to it in 1852. Stahl's efforts went towards - maintaining the integrity of the Lutheran church by insisting on the inviolability of the Augsburg Confession and, in line with this, championing a confederational approach in the face of the pressure towards union. The pressure towards union and towards watering down the confession was unremitting. Twice Stahl felt himself compelled to offer his resignation precisely because of this pressure. Both times the king refused.[124]

Nevertheless, Stahl saw his position in the supreme consistory increasingly being undermined. He complained to minister of culture Raumer about affronts to the Lutherans; in response, he learned that it was Friedrich Wilhelm himself who was driving this policy. And then Stahl found himself being blamed by Leopold von Gerlach for his lack of effectiveness in fighting for the position of Lutherans in the church. However, his inaction was not to blame for this lack of effectiveness; he was simply being sidelined. Again he offered the king his resigna-

---

[124]Nabrings, 139ff.

tion. This time, Friedrich Wilhelm asked him to attend in person the upcoming conference of the Evangelical Alliance, from which the king was hoping for an impulse of revival to the Prussian church. Stahl responded that it was not the conference which inspired his request, but internal church affairs. Not long after this, the king became ill with the sickness from which he never recovered; Stahl's resignation therefore hung in the air for some time. A year later, in 1858, the regent, the future Kaiser Wilhelm I, released him from his position. The process of unification at the cost of confession, which Stahl had fought so hard to forestall, had become reality, and Stahl found no place for himself in church leadership.[125]

Besides the supreme consistory, Stahl also remained active in the annual church assemblies, the first of which had been held in Wittenberg in 1848. Stahl's activity in the annual assembly was twofold: to hinder the effort of church unification in Prussia by pursuing a confederational agenda, and to exert influence in key issues such as the separation of church and state (dealt with in the assemblies of 1849 and 1850), the relationship with the Roman Catholic church (1852), the place of the confessions (1853), and church discipline, along with the question of the philosophy of scientific materialism (1856).[126]

The assembly of 1852 is of interest in that it shows Stahl's catholic spirit in an age when Christians of all stripes needed to join together to face down the threat from the Revolution. The Jesuit order had been allowed to reinitiate mission work in Protestant states of Germany. At the conference, the thesis initially was proposed that Protestants should not overempha-

---

[125]Nabrings, 141.
[126]Nabrings, 134.

size the danger of such missions, and that the real enemy was not Rome but unbelief. Strong objections were raised to this line of thought. Some speakers even referred to Rome as that "monster from Hell," urging the assembly to confront with irreconcilable hatred the "infernal system of the Papacy." As president of the assembly, Stahl took the floor at the conclusion of debate, warning of such condemnation of the Catholic church. He did not wish to burn any bridges. He was able to gain the assembly's assent; in the event, a resolution was passed simply calling on governments not to give up their right of supervision over the churches, Catholic included.[127]

In the question of the church confessions, dealt with in the assembly of 1853, Stahl argued for maintaining the Augsburg Confession as the common confession of the German church. This was accompanied by explanatory statements from each of the three churches, the Lutheran, the Reformed, and the Union. Stahl provided the statement for the Lutherans, a statement highlighting the differences between the Lutheran and Reformed churches; he wished to avoid the slightest implication that unity was to be achieved by dropping controversial points.[128]

The convention of the Evangelical Alliance in Berlin in 1857 was for Stahl an indication of a change in Friedrich Wilhelm's course regarding the church. Stahl and the conservatives staunchly opposed the assembly; Friedrich Wilhelm therefore sought to sideline them by favoring their ecclesiastical oppo-

---

[127]Nabrings, 135.

[128]Nabrings, 135-136. Nabrings' reproach that in this Stahl proved more "tolerant" to the Catholic church than to the Reformed church, does not make sense. Stahl only insisted on recognizing the conflicts as well as the common ground between the churches. Church unity gained at the expense of giving up convictions is useless, was Stahl's viewpoint.

nents. For his part, Stahl saw in this course another attempt at the pursuit of unification at the expense of confession. The annual national Protestant assembly was held in the wake of this convention. Here, one of Friedrich Wilhelm's spokesmen, Bunsen, spoke in favor of a practical ecumenism which would extend even to the Catholic church. Stahl spoke in opposition to Bunsen, viewing his proposals as another attempt to attain church unity at the expense of doctrine. During his speech Stahl was repeatedly interrupted, forcing him to put the assembly before the choice either of letting him continue or of having him resign his position in the presidency. He was able to continue; but he never again would take the floor at an annual assembly. In 1861, he formally resigned his position.[129]

At the pastoral conference in Berlin in 1857, Stahl elaborated on his opposition to the Evangelical Alliance. He considered its characterization as "the community of the saints" to be suspect, as this excluded Catholics. Only God knew the community of the saints; no earthly institution could claim this title for itself. Its avowed goal, to function as the union of evangelical Christians, was problematic in that its assemblies only extended to those persons present and not the churches themselves; it thus was setting itself up as a church. Furthermore, its tendency was toward increasing the separation between church and state.[130]

Stahl's disaffection with the direction in which ecclesiastical affairs were headed reached a climax in his book *The Lutheran Church and the Union: A Scientific Discussion of the Contemporary Question*. Here once and for all he renounced the direction to-

---

[129]Nabrings, 136-137.
[130]Nabrings, 142-143.

ward synodal unification he had cautiously advocated in 1847. The trend toward unification had been unmasked as an effort at achieving unity at the expense of doctrinal consistency; furthermore, unification had become a *fait accompli* and Stahl realized his hopes had been dashed. His book therefore warned not only of the fatal effects such a course would have not only on the Lutheran but also on the Reformed church, but it also functioned as a witness: "Stahl's book on the Union not only is a treatment of a special church-political problem but at the same time a witness to the outsider's role Stahl, and with him the strict confessionalists, assumed with regard to church-political events at the end of the 1850s." As was to be expected, the book met with an undividedly adverse response. Liberalism was triumphant.[131]

Stahl was accused of intolerance toward non-Lutherans, but as is usually the case, such charges masked the real issue. The Calvinist Dutchman Guillaume Groen van Prinsterer – no Lutheran, he – viewed Stahl's work in a different light:

> In 1859 Stahl wrote *The Lutheran Church and the Union.* There he opposes the Union, established in 1817 by royal decree, insofar as it, in his view, threatens the rights and the honor of the Lutheran church. With regard to the Reformed he is brotherly-minded and expresses himself with satisfaction regarding Calvin, Calvinism, the meritoriousness of the Reformed churches in their zeal for martyrdom and noble spirit of liberty. What he actually warns for is the *dogmatophobia* not entirely unknown in the Netherlands either, which in the end admits into the church the most complete skepticism as a by no means unimportant creed of belief or unbelief.... Stahl reminds his readers, in the midst of the vehemence of the confessional conflict which in Germany has relegated

---

[131]Nabrings, 125.

brotherly love to the background, that confessional faithfulness does not rule out living sympathy for the Catholic Christian Church and for the community of the saints, but much rather presupposes it.[132]

An interesting term, that: dogmatophobia. And it exactly captures the essence of the problem. Those pursuing union and evangelical ecumenicity were pursuing it not least as a means to replace dogma and doctrine with a religion of love and emotion, a tendency which is all too visible even to this day. "Stahl resisted the attempts at unification on the part of Unionists and proponents of the Evangelical Alliance, which actually were based on the negative method of attributing un-importance to the deviations of others."[133]

Several other works of Stahl's deserve mention in passing at this point. His book entitled *Protestantism as a Political Principle*, published in 1853, defended Protestantism from the charge brought by Catholics that it was the Reformation that was the true source of the Revolution. On the contrary, Stahl argued, the Reformation provided the most solid basis for a true con-servatism, because it grounded historic right in eternal justice; a conservatism lacking in a transcendent basis was mere reac-tion. Therefore tradition, the heart of Catholicism, was insuffi-cient.

> Hence Protestantism contains a peculiar principle of education and outlook which is decisive to the public (political) condition of the peoples, distinguished from the Catholic and yet in opposition to the rationalistic and the revolutionary. A power of examination, of criticism, not outside of and over the given truth but in the

---

[132]Groen van Prinsterer, *Ter Nagedachtenis van Stahl*, 3-4.
[133]Fafié, 97.

highest given truth, a recognition of historical continuity but always under the higher standard of the eternal command. The entire world-shaping power of Protestantism, its influence on institutions and education, therefore rests on this,… that the factors of the eternal kingdom of God are high above and to be sharply distinguished from all temporal mediation and institution. It is an effluence of justification by faith alone.[134]

Another of his short works, a pamphlet entitled *What is the Revolution* (1852), gained general attention (or notoriety, as the case may be), and was even published in Dutch.[135]

His pamphlet *On Christian Toleration*, published in 1857, was milder in tone than the book discussing tolerance he had published in 1847, *The Christian State in its Relation to Judaism and Deism*. The difference is, in 1847 his ideas had met with some modest agreement; in 1857, they became the subject of bitter dispute. That in itself is a telling sign as to how much times had changed.

An era was ending: of that, everyone was in agreement. "No one could then conceal from himself that an entire age was coming to an end. Leopold von Gerlach wrote in his diary on March 2nd 1856, the first anniversary of the death of Czar Nicholas, that with him an epoch had concluded, and continued: 'That will be the case in much greater degree with King Friedrich Wilhelm IV; all those medieval traditions will end with him.'"[136]

The passing of the age was indeed summed up in the passing of Friedrich Wilhelm IV; "he departed the stage at the

---

[134]Stahl, *Der Protestantismus als politisches Prinzip*, 88.
[135]Fafié, 37.
[136]Schoeps, *Preussen: Geschichte eines Staates*, 235.

proper time."[137] He was struck with debilitating illness in October 1857, and was forced to accede to a regency government led by his brother Wilhelm. His condition continued to deteriorate over the next few years, and he passed away in January 1861.

The passing of the age was more than merely symbolized in Friedrich Wilhelm's departure, for it was through his monarchy that the forces of conservatism had maintained themselves against the onslaught of the Revolution. With the new regency government came a new approach to affairs of church and state. Wilhelm made this plain in an address to the ministers in his newly formed government on November 8, 1858, one month before Stahl was officially released from his position in the supreme consistory. Wilhelm announced the dawning of a "New Era." Henceforth religion would no longer be used as a cover for political ambitions. Orthodoxy, which had become nearly all-powerful in the church, was incompatible with the basic teachings of Christianity and led to hypocrisy. "The coherence of church and state pursued by Friedrich Wilhelm IV and his sacral concept of kingship was rejected in favor of a more realistic approach to politics. In Wilhelm's view, state power was essentially military might and not an authority given by God for rule over earthly relations." The move away from the religious basis of the state was paralleled by strengthening liberalism which pushed aside the Christian conservative ideal.[138]

The realization that a new age had dawned shines through Stahl's address in memoriam of Friedrich Wilhelm IV, spoken at the Berlin pastors' conference on March 18, 1861. Friedrich

---

[137]Schoeps, *Preussen: Geschichte eines Staates*, 235.
[138]Nabrings, 214.

Wilhelm's reign "was not borne by happiness. It was the course of the patient Christian sufferer. Its lot was hostility, misunderstanding, slander, and ingratitude from all sides."[139] From his father he "inherited a crown without equal, highly regarded by the outside world, unweakened internally, still radiant in the glory of the war of liberation." But he also inherited "tasks and entanglements of the thorniest solution, if any."

The worst of it all was "the expansion and height which the ideas of the French Revolution had attained in the 25 years since the Restoration. By then they had gone into all German countries, through all levels of the population. They unceasingly struck the ear in science, in the newspapers, numbing the senses, captivating hearts. In themselves they grew from liberal and democratic ideas to communistic ones, and this excited the masses; the coinage of nationalities was issued alongside the coinage of human rights, and this also corrupted the noble and the wise." Prussia was not spared; far from it. "In Prussia especially, unbelief and revolution were conducted in the name of Protestantism and the Protestant states, thus filling completely the measure of confusion."[140]

Friedrich Wilhelm dedicated his reign to combating this force, with uneven success. His conservative supporters oftentimes were as critical of his actions as his liberal enemies. It was not given to him to gain the victory over the Revolution; but "where his intentions did not succeed against the force of destruction against which he made war, he at least broke off its

---

[139]Stahl, "In memory of His Majesty, the Most Blessed King Friedrich Wilhelm IV and his Reign," published in *Siebzehn parliamentarische Reden*, 265-278.

[140]Stahl, *Siebzehn parliamentarische Reden*, 267.

stinger."[141] He was able to restore the church on a sound basis, restore Christian education, restore many institutions on their Christian basis. And he did this while extending toleration to those who did not share his Christian faith. "In this manner he fulfilled his mission in the world, not in its perfection but in its truth, not in triumphal procession but in patience and perseverance, not in battles against armed might but in unshakeable courage against the whole spiritual power of his age."[142]

The revolution of 1848: was it not a legitimate expression of the popular desire for self-government? Certainly, there are plausible reasons for revolting against an unjust regime: "When a people rises up against utter tyranny, either because of infringement of life, property, women's honor, as with the Greeks under Turkish rule, or because of the overthrow of a historically preserved and guaranteed constitution, as with the English under James II, or because of the persecution of a holy God-bound faith, like the Huguenots, while there is no justification for it to be found in God's Word, no man may set himself up as judge over it." What was the case in Prussia? "Was there in Prussia such a tyranny of this kind? Were there conditions here like those which preceded the French Revolution? Where in Prussia was rule by royal paramours? Where the granting of privileges to the nobility which demeaned the citizenry and closed career paths to it? Where was the clergy consuming the yield of the land in excess? Where were the large landlords sucking the people dry?" If these were not present, there must have been *some* reason to revolt: "the tyranny must then have consisted in the fact that Christianity had not yet been entirely weeded out in favor of philosophy, or that the

---

[141]Stahl, *Siebzehn parliamentarische Reden*, 276.
[142]Stahl, *Siebzehn parliamentarische Reden*, 277.

king did not yield his crown to the people having come of age, or that his ministers had not found the philosopher's stone to solve the problem of pauperism."[143] Reason indeed!

But this lack of a rationale was not the worst part of the revolution of 1848; far worse was the fact that its source was "the most inward fundamental release from the duty of obedience and allegiance to the God-ordained government. Therefore, the guilt of those days, which cannot be expunged from Prussian history, attaches less to the vulgar mass, which, incited to risk from inurement and need, carried out the deed, than to the cultured circles, the educators and bearers of the persuasion in which it had its origin."[144] The revolution of 1848 was not a revolution against oppression or in favor of restoring violated rights; it was a revolution against Christian government, rule by the grace of God, and therefore a continuation of the French Revolution itself.

It was the spirit of the age against which Friedrich Wilhelm fought, a spirit dead-set upon overthrowing the Christian basis of the state. And he would have none of it. "Precisely because he sought the entirety of God-bound orders and ethical goods, he was the true standard-bearer against the apostasy of the age. Well might another ruler than he maintain with iron rule the unrestricted princely power and the unchanged existing order, strike down the uprisings of the people, put his foot on the neck of the movement toward freedom. Even so, such a ruler could not equal the King of Prussia." For herein did not lie the apostasy of the times: "He was the true standard-bearer against the apostasy of the times, because he recognized the seeds of the apostasy also in the sins of the government, in the poor

---

[143]Stahl, *Siebzehn parliamentarische Reden*, 268-269.
[144]Stahl, *Siebzehn parliamentarische Reden*, 269.

example of the princes, in Machiavellian politics of expansion, in the suppression of spiritual life, in bureaucratic withering, in hierarchical pressure exercised by the church, in profane pressure exercised against the church."[145]

Truly Stahl here laid bare the essence of the apostasy in both Prussia and Europe as a whole. The government itself was being reshaped in the image of the Revolution, and the fruits could not be better summed up than in this list. The true church oppressed, the false church an instrument of oppression; bureaucracy sucking the sap out of society; elites taking the lead in setting a bad example; the pursuit of the politics of expansion and hegemony. This was what Stahl, Friedrich Wilhelm, and the true conservatives were fighting against, underneath the surface phenomena of monarchical vs. popular sovereignty.

It was not long after delivering this speech that Stahl himself was called home to his Lord. "On August 8 Stahl and his wife arrived in Bad Brückenau in the attempt to find healing for the afflictions which had affected him for so long, but which he had suffered in silence. The baths, unfortunately, brought him no relief: when an infirmity overcame Stahl, the summoned doctor could offer no further assistance. Following a short death struggle, during which time the patient remained fully alert, the man whose strong spirit had inhabited a fragile body passed away on August 10th 1861."[146] His death made a deep impression. The funeral was conducted on August 19th in the Church of St. Matthew. The procession included Prince Albert of Prussia, ministers and former ministers, court

---

[145]Stahl, *Siebzehn parliamentarische Reden*, 266-267.
[146]Fafié, 39.

Kreuzzeitung, January 3rd 1861, announcing the death of Friedrich Wilhelm IV.

preachers, university professors and flag officers, who accompanied the widow and Stahl's brother, a professor at Erlangen
University. The monument marking his grave was a modest
one. "Centrally placed on a white marble rosy cross is an image
of Christ's head with the crown of thorns. The inscription
reads: Fr. J. Stahl – 16 Jan. 1802-10 Aug. 1861. Wer mich be-
kennt vor den Menschen, den will ich auch bekennen vor
meinem Vater."[147]

That is: he who acknowledges Me before men, I will also
acknowledge before my Father.

---

[147]Fafié, 39-40.

8. Blood and Iron

And so passed the age of Christian conservatism in Prussia. Stahl's departure was not the only one mourned among Christian conservatives at this time. Leopold von Gerlach, Friedrich Wilhelm's adjutant and the brother of the aforementioned Ludwig, died from exposure nine days after Friedrich Wilhelm: during the funeral procession he had followed after the casket, exposed to the elements, head bared, helmet clasped in hand; as Bismarck put it, he had accompanied his lord's body into the grave like an old Germanic warrior. Savigny, the father of the Historical School of Law, died on October 25, 1861. Conservative stalwart L.G. von Thile passed on August 24; Carl von Voß a bit later, on February 3, 1864.[148]

The reign of Friedrich Wilhelm was now shown to have been but an interim. A struggle was taking place in Prussia, mirroring the struggle which had been Germany's peculiar burden since the Middle Ages: that of the choice between the common interests of the broader German nation, and indeed Christendom, and the narrow interests of the Prussian state. Throughout its history, Prussia had been torn between holding up its end of the Holy Roman Empire and pursuing its own interests over against the interests of that Empire. That conflict burst into the open in the reign of Frederick II, "the Great," who openly defied the Empire and its Habsburg emperor by engaging in blatant territorial aggrandizement, to wit, by invad-

---

[148]Schoeps, *Preussen: Geschichte eines Staates*, 236.

Wilhelm I

ing and conquering the Habsburg possession Silesia in
1740. This mode of foreign policy
came to be known as
"Fredericianism;" upon Frederick II's death at the eve of
the French Revolution it went
into abeyance, as the locus of
will-to-power shifted back to
France, this time in its Revolutionary mode. But it continued to slumber under the surface.

Meanwhile, the "New
Age" which dawned upon the
demise of Friedrich Wilhelm IV petered out into a dreary stale-
mate between Crown and Parliament. What had ostensibly -
begun with so much promise had degenerated into the familiar
conflict between the rights of the crown and the rights of the
assembly. Only this time, there was no Stahl to propose mod-
erating, statesmanlike solutions.

The conflict focused on the army, that venerable pillar of
Prussian monarchical supremacy. King Wilhelm was desirous
of upgrading the capacities of the army, especially its ability
quickly to mobilize; it had been found wanting in previous
emergencies, such as the crisis of 1850. He wished to increase
the periods of enlistment as well as those of reserve commitment. He furthermore wished to increase its size to bring it in
line with the increase in population. The assembly rejected the
proposal out of hand; for its part, the government argued that
the assembly had no right to do so, the army being under the
direct authority of the king. A provisional solution was found

in the assembly's approving a temporary budget for one year. But the question of the size of the army and law of conscription remained unresolved.

New elections were held in December 1861, resulting in the resounding triumph of the new German Progressive Party, composed of both liberals and democrats. This new party became the largest in the lower house. It refused to accept the government's proposed army legislation. It also demanded control over the army's budget. The government, of course, would not stand for that: a right of refusing the army's budget would be tantamount to a right to control over the army, and that was the king's province.

Wilhelm soon prorogued the parliament, in March 1862. The move backfired; the new chamber proved to be even more liberal than the previous one, even less amenable to negotiation. The situation came to a head. Either the parliament would gain control, as in England, or the crown would force its prerogative. No compromise was possible.

By now Wilhelm had arrived at his wit's end. For a time he toyed with the idea of abdicating in favor of his son, who was of more liberal views and would accommodate himself to parliamentary desires. Historians like to speculate on what would have happened had this indeed come to pass. Instead, on the advice of war minister Roon, Wilhelm had Otto von Bismarck, at the time Prussia's ambassador in Paris, recalled to Berlin. Soon thereafter, Wilhelm appointed Bismarck as Minister President.

It was a move Wilhelm had postponed for the longest time, until he came to the conclusion that no one else could help him out of this untenable situation. Bismarck was mistrusted by liberal and conservative alike. His anti-Austrian views were viewed with profound misgivings by conservatives. And his methodology, already in evidence early on, was cause for serious concern. In a speech to the lower house during the crisis of 1850, he had stated unequivocally: "the only sound basis for a large state is statist egotism."[149] Ludwig von Gerlach, Bismarck's mentor early in his career and the co-leader with Stahl of the conservative fraction in Parliament, in 1853 warned that Bismarck easily might fall into the trap of "worldliness" and "the Satan."[150]

Friedrich Wilhelm, the story is told, had tagged Bismarck as the "red reactionary;" he "smells of blood, only to be used when the bayonet rules."[151] Wilhelm was likewise ill-disposed to the Junker squire, but recognized in Bismarck a personality who could save his throne. But at what price?

For his part, Bismarck realized that Wilhelm was close to throwing in the towel. The moment of truth came on the famous meeting on October 4, 1862, in the royal train. Wilhelm was returning from spending time with his wife, his son the crown prince, and other notables, all of whom were deeply troubled by his choice of leader. Bismarck could guess what their conversation had been like: "talk of Louis XVI, Strafford, Polignac;" all martyrs in the cause of royalism.[152]

Pflanze recounts the story:

> Anxiously [Bismarck] hurried out to meet the royal train returning from the south on October 4. Boarding at Jüterbog, he found William alone and morose in an ordinary first-class compartment. "I foresee exactly how all this is going to end," the Hohenzoller declared. "Out there in the Opernplatz under my

---

[149]Schoeps, *Bismarck*, 142.
[150]Schoeps, *Das andere Preußen*, 23.
[151]quoted in A. J. P. Taylor, *Bismarck: The Man and the Statesman*, 26.
[152]Pflanze, *Bismarck and the Development of Germany*, 175.

windows they will cut off your head and a little later mine." Carefully Bismarck chose his ground. What better fate than to die for such a cause — "I in the struggle for the cause of my king and your majesty for the rights which are yours by the grace of God?" William should think of the noble death of Charles I, not the ignominious end of Louis XVI. "Your majesty is faced with the necessity of fighting. You cannot capitulate. You must oppose tyranny, even if you incur bodily danger."[153]

Bismarck's fighting words reinvigorated the scion of the proud ruling house of Hohenzollern. From that point, Wilhelm stood behind Bismarck as he carried out government policy in the teeth of parliamentary resistance. Public opinion was foursquare against the government, but that mattered not, not in Prussia — the army remained loyal.

The king's support provided Bismarck the platform to carry out the plans he had been brewing ever since he had served as Prussian representative to the German Confederation in Frankfurt in the 1850s. There he had hatched the notion of supplanting Austria as the leading power in Germany and forging a unified German nation with Prussia at its heart. Wilhelm had not brought Bismarck into the government for this, but only to maintain his throne in the face of domestic attack. But in Bismarck Wilhelm had gotten a jack-in-the-box who would pop out with all manner of schemes that were not part of the original bargain.

To attain his ends, Bismarck had recourse to the Frederician tradition that still lurked in the subconscious of the Prussian despite its years of suppression under the regimes of Friedrich Wilhelm III and IV. Bismarck knew that the domestic conflict could be solved by achieving successes in foreign policy, suc-

---

[153]Pflanze, *Bismarck and the Development of Germany*, 175.

cesses advancing the cause of Prussia in the world.

> Since reconciliation had failed and capitulation was unthink-
> able, ways had to be found to overcome the parliamentary opposi-
> tion. More than a year before his appointment as minister-presi-
> dent Bismarck had outlined to Roon what his tactic would be in
> this situation. The crown, he wrote, could disengage itself within
> only by a successful diversion without. "For fourteen years we
> have cultivated the taste of the nation for politics without satisfy-
> ing its appetite, and hence it seeks nourishment in the gutter. We
> are almost as vain as the French. If we can persuade ourselves of
> our importance abroad, we are willing to let many things at home
> go by the board."[154]

The first step on this road was taken during the so-called
Schleswig-Holstein crisis. These were two duchies under Dan-
ish rule; Schleswig, though, harbored a large German population, and Holstein was a member of the German Confederation. Conflict arose when the king of Denmark died, prompt-
ing a German prince, Friedrich von Augustenburg, to dispute
succession to the duchies. The conflict inflamed German nationalist impulses. Bismarck rode this wave of patriotism, not
to secure Schleswig-Holstein for Prince Friedrich, thus creating
another German Confederation member state, but to annex
the duchies to Prussia. By a combination of adroitness, cun-
ning, and patience, he laid the groundwork for this eventuality.

Bismarck was also busy whittling away at the royal conscience. Annexation was something Wilhelm had to get used
to. Perhaps he realized how far Bismarck was leading him away
from the example his brother had set.

---

[154]Pflanze, *Bismarck and the Development of Germany*, 176-177.

On February 3, 1864, only two days after the invasion of Schleswig, Bismarck began to shove forward the alternative of annexation. In a crown council he openly confessed that this was his ultimate goal. "I reminded the king that each of his immediate forebears, except his brother, had won for the state an increase in territory... and encouraged him to do the same." But the Hohenzoller was troubled. To the protocol which recorded the discussion he added that annexation was not the objective of Prussian policy, but merely a possible outcome of the affair. Honest William needed time to get accustomed to the idea and more arguments to square it with his conscience.[155]

The Schleswig-Holstein issue was but the tip of iceberg of the potential of German nationalism. For Bismarck, nationalism had replaced conservatism as the ideological foundation of monarchy. In his conflict with Austria, he exploited it to the full. Austria was at the head of a multinational empire; nationalism was precisely what could destroy it as a unified polity. Knowing this, Bismarck encouraged nationalist movements in the various member nations of the Austro-Hungarian Empire. The encouragement of nationalism both helped Prussia in its project of German unification and hurt Austria in its bid simply to hold together.

Bismarck had become the revolutionary, the proponent of popular sovereignty. In the service of his liege lord, he was bent on shaking the throne of Austria, but not only that one. Standing in the way of his plan for Prussian-led unification was not only Austria but the other sovereign heads leading the various states of Germany. In his view, "the 'sovereignty' of the lesser states was an 'unhistorical, Godless, and unjust swindle'

---

[155]Pflanze, *Bismarck and the Development of Germany*, 246.

dangerous to the future of Prussia and Germany."[156] In essence, the monarchical legitimism that once was the cornerstone of German conservatism had been transformed in Bismarck's policy into the chief stumbling block in the way of Prussia achieving its ambitions. It was a reversal of Jesus's saying: the chief cornerstone had become the stone that was rejected.

Bismarck's revolution took a step further when he managed to maneuver Austria into war while keeping France and Russia neutral. The battle of Königgrätz (July 3, 1866) marked the end of hundreds of years of history in which Austria had taken the lead in Germany. Henceforth, Prussia had the upper hand. Austria withdrew from the field, leaving the lesser German states to fend for themselves in the face of the Prussian juggernaut.

Bismarck actually was rather lenient with most of the other German states, nearly all of whom had chosen Austria's side in the war. He did however annex Hanover, Nassau, Hesse-Kassel, Schleswig-Holstein, and Frankfurt am Main, and formed a North German Confederation of the German states located above the Main River. The south German states he hoped to win over rather than conquer.

Here again, the going was slow as the remaining states, headed up by Bavaria, were anything but keen on acceding to Prussian hegemony. So Bismarck resorted to his time-honored method, war against an external enemy, to gin up patriotic fervor which he hoped would spill over into political unification.

France was the unlucky victim this time. Bismarck had little trouble in maneuvering the weak Louis Napoleon into a war.

---

[156]Pflanze, *Bismarck and the Development of Germany*, 146.

The details make for rather sordid reading.[157] "Bismarck... bears all the responsibility of a calm, intelligent man who deliberately eggs on an excited, ignorant one to begin a bloody quarrel."[158] Success on the battlefield was followed by adulation from erstwhile opponents. "As Bismarck anticipated, war with France produced an upsurge of German national feeling which helped to fill the chasm of time. In sharing the same dangers, experiences, and hatreds the Germans established a psychological bond which, if it did not extinguish, at least diminished, the significance of the tribal sentiments, dynastic loyalties, customs, and mores which had previously divided them."[159] The crowning moment came when Wilhelm was crowned Kaiser of the newly-minted Second German Empire, something into which he himself had to be pushed by Bismarck. From every angle one looks at it, the new Empire was the product of the Iron Chancellor's sheer force of will.

Otto von Bismarck

The pillars of the Prussian throne, Pflanze notes, had been the dynastic loyalty, Prussian nationalism, the Junker aristocracy, the army, and the bureaucracy; Bismarck added the pillar of German nationalism.[160] What Pflanze fails to mention was

---

[157]An incisive narrative of events is contained in Anderson *et al.*, *The Roots of the War*, 3ff.

[158]*Ibid.*, 6.

[159]Pflanze, *Bismarck and the Development of Germany*, 482.

[160]Pflanze, *Bismarck and the Development of Germany*, 297-298.

the Christian religion, which had been a pillar as well but had now been *replaced* by German nationalism.

Bismarck had been a card-carrying member of the conservative party led by Stahl. He had been furthered in his career by the conservatives, especially the Gerlach brothers. He had converted to Christianity in 1846, and it was this newfound faith along with marriage to the pious Johanna von Puttkamer that had brought him within the Christian conservative circle. So he was well-acquainted with the views and policies advocated by this group, and indeed with Friedrich Wilhelm IV himself.

The trouble is, what they viewed as restraint in the name of higher ethical principles, the major one of which was authority by the grace of God – the principle of legitimism – he came to view as pious hogwash.[161] His change of heart is chronicled in the exchange of letters with Leopold von Gerlach that he included in his memoirs.[162] Bismarck turned his back completely on the policies and principles of the reign of Friedrich Wilhelm IV, which had only, he felt, served to hold back Prussia from its rightful place of leadership and hegemony. Tellingly, under a letter from Ludwig von Gerlach dated May 25th 1864, Bismarck scribbled in pencil, "Old Jesuit pater!"[163]

Bismarck reestablished the venerable Lutheran shortcoming of the divorce between piety and politics, relegating religion to the private sphere and abandoning the public sphere to the play of interests, of *Realpolitik:* a Lutheranism which Stahl and the other Christian conservative leaders had abandoned in

---

[161]He apparently made an exception for the throne which he himself served, that of the Hohenzollerns.

[162]Bismarck, *Bismarck, the Man & the Statesman,* 171ff.

[163]Schoeps, *Bismarck über Zeitgenossen – Zeitgenossen über Bismarck,* 154.

favor of a full-orbed public Christianity. Wittingly or unwittingly, he reawakened the lust for Germanic gods that had always slumbered in the hearts of good Germans.

> We must ask ourselves how the German people came to give first Bismarck and then Hitler their opportunities. Indeed, how did they come to raise Bismarck and Hitler to idols? Because they have tended to worship force, because they consider every kind of inconsiderateness, especially in the military field and in domestic and foreign policy, to be proof of increased strength, so that the borderline of brutality becomes fluid; in short, because they are always impressed by the cavalryman's boot and a fist banged upon the table.... Straight through the soul and conscience of the Germans runs the uncertain frontier between the Christian West and barbarism, said Quariglia, the Italian anti-fascist, during the last war. What is worst is that so many among us have always been proud of our participation in barbarism, even before Hegel, then particularly after Nietzsche, and all the way down to Ernst Jünger. Barbarian or Christian? We ought to put that query to Bismarck, we must address it above all to every German. Unfortunately, Heinrich Heine was not far wrong when he expressed the opinion that Christianity had only thinly and temporarily tamed the barbarian instincts of the Germans. We must add as well the Prussian-German faculty for having simultaneously a private Christianity and a deliberately heathenish public policy which, as we saw, could call up old Thor or Donar.[164]

The politics of Bismarck were the politics of the Anti-Christ, argued Ludwig von Gerlach. "The Ten Commandments – he cannot bear them!"[165]

---

[164]Alfred von Martin, "Bismarck and Ourselves: a Contribution to the Destruction of an Historical Legend," in Kohn, *German History: Some New German Views,* 100.

[165]Quoted in Schoeps, *Das andere Preußen,* p. 66.

That Hanover, Nassau, Frankfurt, Electoral Hesse were devoured by Bismarck entirely in accordance with the law of the jungle [den Regeln der Naturgeschichte], I do not have the slightest doubt. My pain is no sentimental pain, that Hanover, Nassau and Frankfurt no longer exist, but the pain of a Prussian, German Christian, that my party and my fatherland Prussia so shamefully have violated the Ten Commandments, and by the vice of pseudo-patriotism have done damage to their souls and corrupted their consciences.[166]

"For the commandments of Christian ethics as represented by von Gerlach, Bismarck appears factually as the 'Antichrist,' the more so because he can justifiably be impugned for embellishing with Christianity his robber politics by special days of fasting and prayer, chorales and the like, which not even Friedrich II or Napoleon did."[167]

For Gerlach's troubles, he was cast into the outer darkness of political oblivion. Nearly all his erstwhile friends and colleagues turned away from him in favor of a newfound faith, Bismarckianism. The newspaper which he cofounded and for which he wrote for 18 years, the *Kreuzzeitung*, showed him the door for writing an editorial critical of Bismarck's imminent war against Austria.

Gerlach had lived on to see the evil day which Stahl and the others had dreaded. That it had come through one of their own was doubly painful. Bismarck had simply not understood Germany's unique calling in the world. "The German nation is not to be merely national in the same sense as the French and the English nation," Gerlach argued, "As such the German essentially is not merely the member of a nation in

---

[166]Quoted in Schoeps, *Bismarck*, p. 147.
[167]Schoeps, *Das andere Preußen*, 66.

contradistinction to other nations, but a world citizen, a fellow of the kingdom of God, in a different sense than other Christians. The Kingdom of God is his fatherland." Therefore this one-sided nationalism would not only result in the downfall of Germany but the downfall of Christendom as well. The Germanic could only develop if it first stood in connection with Christianity. The German's predilection to world citizenship, which perceives strict nationality as a straitjacket, predisposes him to represent the Christian idea of empire. "The peculiar glory of the German nation ever consists in subordinating national interests to universal, human religious-churchly interests. Is this people now to have an exclusive, petty national consciousness foisted upon it?"[168]

Bismarck had betrayed the very foundations of conservatism. He had exchanged Christianity as the source of law for a base utilitarianism. "'Nothing succeeds like success.' This is an American saying, probably of slight ethical value. During the next decades, however, it made Bismarck seem the king of all statesmen."[169] He had seduced Germany into exchanging its historical, supra-national calling as the protector of Christianity and the Church for power-oriented nationalism. And what bitter fruit from this fatal triumph of the Revolution principle awaited harvesting.[170]

---

[168]Quoted in Schoeps, *Das andere Preußen*, 47-48.

[169]Anderson *et al.*, *The Roots of the War*, 6.

[170]For more on the centrality of Germany to the course of world history, see Alvarado, *A Common Law*.

9. A Prophetic Witness

The import of Stahl's life and work can be summed up in the impromptu statement that became his trademark: "authority, not majority." Stahl early on came to the conviction that what was at stake in the French Revolution, and the struggle both for and against that revolution, was the very concept of authority; and that liberty itself was completely dependent upon the maintenance of authority. Authority, not majority, i.e., expressed collective will, established the framework of social order. Authority did not depend upon the human will for its legitimacy, it existed prior to human will, and in fact conditioned that will. Human choice is constrained by the structure of authority that it finds around it, and it must operate within the parameters set by that authority. It cannot set itself above that authority, or it will destroy authority. And the vacuum that the destruction of authority creates will be filled by despotism.

If the source of authority is not the human will, then what is? Stahl's answer is clear, and it explains why he put all his eggs in one basket, as it were: the Christian religion provides the legitimacy for authority that exists anterior to the human will. Stahl's struggle was the struggle first and foremost for the maintenance of Christianity as the standard of public order. He fought tooth and nail against the trend toward privatizing Christianity in favor of a public neutrality vis-a-vis religion. For this he was castigated as a Pietist, Jesuit papist, and worse. But his goal was not to foist Christianity upon those unwilling to accept it. His goal was to maintain the Christian character of public life in order to maintain intact those authority structures. In turn, those authority structures were not ends in themselves; they enabled the growth of liberty extending to all members of society, not only believing Christians. Put simply, Christianity was necessary to the maintenance of that venerable goal, liberty and justice for all. Through the Christian religion, honor and respect is maintained for all those in authority, from the king to the meanest head of a household.

For this reason, Stahl put all the blame for the degeneration of the social order in Europe on liberalism. "Yes, Gentlemen," he argued in the People's House, in the speech that called forth such wonderment from his opponents (see p. 65 above), "I will go even farther. The danger to our Fatherland and the existence of state institutions does not come from the *democratic side*, but from the *side of the liberals* (enthusiastic bravo from the right)." The liberals view themselves as the only progressive, enlightened group, the justified, the respectable, the group that no one could or dared contradict without being vituperated as an absolutist, a feudalist, or a pietist. "It is from that system and not democracy – which nowadays one wishes to make a scapegoat" – this statement called forth hilarity and calls of Bravo! from the right – "from which the principles and institutions have come that the core of the people in large part now recognize as destructive and will come to recognize as such even more." It was the liberals, now tripping over themselves to affirm the principle of monarchy, who in 1849 had striven to undermine and neutralize monarchy. "We jointly combat the *Revolution*; but the Revolution is not the *act* but the *condition*; it is the condition in which that which by eternal ordinance is to rest at the foundation comes to rest at the top, and vice versa." Revolution is when subjects and subject-assemblies sit in judgment of kings; but when the Bible commands equal justice for the great and the small, it is *not* calling for the subject to sit in judgement over the king. "This is the system of revolution, that it is not the articulated groups of society which hold as the basic right of the nation, but their dissolution; that the promotion of the Christian faith, the education of the future generation in that faith, is not considered as the nation's highest concern but as a matter of indifference, as a mere private affair." This is true revolution, and it always leads to that which everyone recognizes as true revolution, violent overthrow.

"I do not fear the *acute* disease of *democracy* – the organism of the political body in Germany is still strong enough to resist it – I fear the *chronic* disease of *liberalism* (Bravo! from the right). I do not fear *overthrow*, I fear *disintegration*. When the principles and teachings of liberalism come to power and further proliferate, they will erode the entire body politic like mercury in the bones, and I seriously doubt whether, when a second storm arises, we will be able to withstand it."

In standing against the revolutionary movements they have awakened, the liberals are like the sorcerer's apprentice, unable to put a stop to the streams of water they have called forth. "They have forgotten the magic word needed to stop them, or the word is no longer in their lexicon; for this word is *authority* (enthusiastic Bravo from the right). They wished to stop the water with the magic word of their system: "*Majority! Majority!*" But instead of ceasing, the waters kept coming, kept rising, up to their necks, until finally in Vienna and Berlin the appropriate word of authority was invoked, and the ghost vanished in an instant (Bravo from the right)."[171]

Yes, authority, not majority. The disease of liberalism is the

---

[171]Stahl, *Siebzehn parliamentarische Reden*, 160-162.

erosion of pre-existing authority, the submission of authority to referendum, at all levels of the social order from the family to the community to the state. Opinion, individual and collective, becomes the criterion for legitimacy.

The structure of authority as developed by Stahl provided the indispensable framework for the common-law tradition of liberty as developed by Burke and Savigny. Savigny's Historical School championed customary law in opposition to legislation, which it viewed as the top-down imposition of absolute sovereignty. The common law of Germany, like its cousin the common law of England cum America, had developed not out of legislation but through custom as sanctioned by the courts. But such a framework is not in itself sufficient; it requires underpinnings. For the "judge-made" law can easily be manipulated by an activist judiciary. The crying need of a common-law system is a clear acknowledgment of the ground and principle of law – the ultimate source of law, beyond custom and legislation. Stahl provided that criterion in his theory of institutions as the fixed loci of authority in society, in terms of which laws could be developed and enforced. Hence, the family as grounded in traditional marriage provided the framework for the cluster of laws governing the relations of family members amongst themselves and of the family and its head of household over against society at large. Likewise private property, the local community, occupation, church, and state. Monarchy figured largely in Stahl's conception, but only as a function of constitutional government, not as an end in itself.

A basic principle of Stahl's framework was therefore this institutional understanding as a necessary counterpoint to voluntary association, and in fact he saw the two as necessary counterparts, especially in church and state. The church was both institution and congregation, in its institutional aspect set above and beyond participatory government, and in its congregational aspect subject to participatory government. The same framework is seen in his conception of the state. The relation between the two poles was not a static one, but rather one of a sliding scale; as the people become more responsible and capable of self-government, the institutional pole recedes in favor of the congregational/popular pole. But since in Stahl's view the Revolution had corrupted the popular mindset, 19th century Europe and especially Germany were in no condition to put the emphasis on popular government. The indispensable criterion in Stahl's view was the maintenance of the Christian character of the state and of public institutions. Apart from this, there could be no standard of justice and society would disintegrate into a power struggle and despotic rule. This was his conclusion, and who can say, having looked upon the further history of Europe, that he got it wrong?

Stahl's efforts even in practical political terms were not entirely fruitless. After all, it was mainly through his effort that Prussia even gained a constitutional form of government, rudimentary though it was. Without his mediation, Prussia may well have collapsed into some form or other of civil war. As it happened, the constitutional government with its limited role for the elected assembly maintained itself until the catastrophe of the First World War. Of course, that constitutional framework did not provide the capability of withstanding a Bismarck – in this sense, too much power had been put into the hand of the king, a king who in this case could be manipulated into repeated wars for the sake of Prussian reason of state. But this was more the result of the pointed rejection of Christian principles as the lodestar of policy than it was a failure of constitutional mechanism. Mechanism is no substitute for principle.

This yields perhaps the most important lesson for us to glean from Stahl. It is the lesson of the necessity to declare and confess, publicly and constitutionally, the ground of law. If Bismarck had been forced to justify his actions in terms of Christian principles as formulated by the likes of Stahl, he would quickly have had to abandon his efforts. But because the times were ripe for the silencing of public Christianity, and because public opinion uniformly rejected the need for such a confession, there was no standard of justice capable of restraining Bismarck. Reason of state is the lodestar of modern politics, in tandem with the doctrine of human rights. The latter is insufficient as a criterion of justice, and furthermore can be, and is today, used precisely to obstruct the course of justice in the punishment of criminals and rogue nations. Reason of state was Bismarck's criterion. Stahl, in line with Christian conservatives such as Ludwig von Gerlach, championed a community of Christian nations as the continuation of the tradition of the Holy Roman Empire.

Today, there is no clear definition provided with regard to the ground of law. The latest incarnation of justice is simply that which international, unaccountable bodies decide upon. They then turn around and argue violations of their version of international law. It is a travesty of justice to make diplomats and bureaucrats outside of any structure of accountability responsible for legislating to the nations what is right and what is wrong. They continue to be able to do so because peoples and nations have gotten into the habit of regarding this so-called international community as ipso facto a higher arbiter of justice. That this international community can enjoy such elevated status is the result of two world wars caused by the collapse of true international community. But the solution to that collapse is not tyranny by an unelected elite in the name of international law.

The same problem faces the nations internally. This is especially on view in the United States. The absence of a clearly defined ground and basis of law has made constitutional law into a political football, in which policy or even ideological preferences trump justice rather than the other way around. This is a problem of constitutional law. The ground of law has to be stated specifically in the document, otherwise it will imported into it, and all of its stipulations will be twisted or nullified on the basis of that presupposition. Law becomes opinion, the learned opinion of the robed justices, who simply exemplify whatever opinion is fashionable among academics at that particular time.[172]

Authority, not majority. Behind this statement of Stahl's lies another, which illumines it: God's law, not man's. For it is divine law which provides both the legitimation for authority and the delimitation thereof, circumscribing that authority, restricting it to definite bounds. Apart from such a law, there is only opinion. And where there is opinion, there is the struggle for power to impose that opinion, the one upon the other; in the name of tolerance comes the oppressive rule of political correctness. Anarchy breeds despotism, and vice versa. This is the ultimate result of the humanistic view of law and government; and it was the clear realization that such a result must be averted that provided the driving force behind the life and work of Friedrich Julius Stahl.

---

[172]The desire to supplant opinion in favor of truth as the basis of lawmaking is what motivates Plato throughout his *Republic*.

Select Bibliography

Stahl's Major Published Works

Das monarchische Princip: eine staatsrechtlich-politische Abhandlung.
   Heidelberg: Mohr, 1845.

Der christliche Staat und sein Verhältniss zu Deismus und Judenthum.
   Berlin: Oehmigke, 1847

*Der Protestantismus als politisches Princip: Vorträge auf Veranstaltung
   des Evangelischen Vereins für kirchliche Zwecke zu Berlin im
   März 1853 gehalten.* 2nd unrevised ed. Berlin: Schultze,
   1853.

*Die deutsche Reichsverfassung nach Beschlüssen der deutschen
   Nationalversammlung und nach dem Entwurf der drei
   königlichen Regierungen.* Berlin: W. Hertz, 1849.

*Die gegenwärtigen Parteien in Staat und Kirche. Neunundzwanzig
   akademische Vorlesungen.* Berlin: Hertz 1863.

Die Kirchenverfassung nach Lehre und Recht der Protestanten. Erlang-
   en: T. Bläsing, 1840

Die Philosophie des Rechts. 2 volumes. Heidelberg: J.C.B. Mohr:
   1830-1837; 2nd ed. 1845-1847; 3rd ed. 1854-1856.

*Die Revolution und die constitutionelle Monarchie, eine Reihe
   ineinandergreifender Abhandlungen.* 2nd expanded ed. Berlin:
   W. Hertz, 1849.

Siebzehn parlamentarische Reden und drei Vorträge. Berlin: Hertz,
   1862.

*Ueber christliche Toleranz: ein Vortrag, gehalten auf Veranstaltung des
   Evangelischen Vereins für kirchliche Zwecke, am 29. März
   1855.* Berlin: Schultze, 1855.

Zwei Sendschreiben an die Unterzeichner der Erklärung vom 15, beziehungsweise 26 August 1845 zugleich als ein Votum in der Augsburgischen Confessions-Frage. Berlin: Verlag von E. H. Schroeder, 1845.

Major Secondary Sources, annotated

Arnim, Henning von. Introduction to *Die Philosophie des Rechts: 1830-1837: eine Auswahl nach der 5. Auflage (1870)* by Friedrich Julius Stahl. Tübingen: Mohr, 1926.

A pro-Stahl exposition prior to the Nazis coming to power, when Stahl's memory had not yet been entirely expunged.

Barclay, David E. *Frederick William IV and the Prussian Monarchy, 1840-1861.* Oxford: Clarendon Press, 1995.

An exemplary biography and a fine introduction to this period of history in Prussia.

Fafié, Gerard. *Friedrich Julius Stahl: invloeden van zijn leven en werken in Nederland, 1847-1880.* Rotterdam: Bronder-Offset, 1975.

Very helpful summary of Stahl's life and work, in Dutch.

Füßl, Wilhelm. "Friedrich Julius Stahl (1802-1861)." In *Politische Theorien des 19. Jahrhunderts: I. Konservatismus,* ed. Bernd Heidenreich, 187-200. Hessische Landeszentrale für politische Bildung: n.d.

A short summary of Stahl's life and work, in German.

Füßl, Wilhelm. *Professor in der Politik: Friedrich Julius Stahl (1802-1861): das monarchische Prinzip und seine Umsetzung in die parlamentarische Praxis.* Göttingen: Vandenhoeck & Ruprecht, 1988.

A key resource to assessing Stahl's political importance.

The primary source for chapters four and five.

Koglin, Olaf Karl Friedrich. *Die Briefe Friedrich Julius Stahls.* Dissertation, University of Kiel, 1975.

An accessible source to key pieces of Stahl's correspondence, in German.

Masur, Gerhard. *Friedrich Julius Stahl : Geschichte seines Lebens, Aufstieg und Entfaltung, 1802-1840.* Berlin: Mittler, 1930.

The primary source for Stahl's early life, and therefore for the second and third chapters of this book. It was to be followed by a volume 2, which never materialized due to the accession of the Nazis to power.

Nabrings, Arie. *Friedrich Julius Stahl: Rechtsphilosophie und Kirchenpolitik.* Bielefeld: Luther-Verlag, 1983.

A key source to Stahl's ecclesiastical thought and action, in German.

Pflanze, Otto. *Bismarck and the Development of Germany: The Period of Unification, 1815-1871.* Princeton, NJ: Princeton University Press, 1971.

An excellent overview of Bismarck's career as it impinges on the time period covered by this book.

Schoeps, Hans-Joachim. *Bismarck über Zeitgenossen – Zeitgenossen über Bismarck.* Frankfurt a.M., Berlin, Vienna, Ullstein: Ullstein Sachbuch, 1981 [1972].

_____. *Das andere Preußen : konservative Gestalten und Probleme im Zeitalter Friedrich Wilhelm IV.* 5th revised ed. Berlin: Haude & Spener, 1981.

An eye-opening introduction to old-school Prussian conservatism, prior to its being hijacked by Bismarck. Essential reading. In German.

_____. *Preussen : Geschichte eines Staates : Bilder und Zeugnisse.* Frankfurt am Main/Berlin: Verlag Ullstein GmbH,

1981.

An important corrective to the standard, wholly negative view of Prussia in German history, providing a more balanced view of Prussia's role. In German.

Other Secondary Sources

Alvarado, Ruben. *A Common Law: The Law of Nations and Western Civilization.* Aalten, the Netherlands: Pietas Press, 1999.

Anderson, William, William Stearns Davis, and Mason W. Tyler, *The Roots of the War: A Non-Technical History of Europe, 1870-1914 A.D.* New York: Century, 1918.

Bigler, Robert M. *The Politics of German Protestantism: The Rise of the Protestant Church Elite in Prussia, 1815-1848.* Berkeley and Los Angeles: University of California Press, 1972.

Bismarck, Otto von. *Bismarck, the Man & the Statesman: Being the Reflections and Reminiscences of Otto, Prince Von Bismarck,* trans. Butler, A. J., vol. 1 New York: Harper & Brothers, 1899.

Boles Jr., Laurence Huey. *The Huguenots, the Protestant Interest, and the War of the Spanish Succession, 1702-1714.* Unpublished PhD dissertation, Northern Arizona University, 1994.

Burke, Edmund. *Reflections on the Revolution in France. Select Works of Edmund Burke, vol. 2.* Foreword and Biographical Note by Francis Canavan. Indianapolis: Liberty Fund, 1999.

Dietrich, Richard. *Kleine Geschichte Preußens.* Berlin: Haude und Spenersche Verlagsbuchhandlung, 1966.

Drucker, Peter. *Friedrich Julius Stahl: konservative Staatslehre und geschichtliche Entwicklung*. Tübingen: Mohr, 1932.

Eliot, T.S. *The Idea of a Christian Society*. London: Faber and Faber Limited, 1939.

Geyl, Pieter. "Nederlands staatkunde in de Spaanse Successie-oorlog" [Dutch statecraft during the War of the Spanish Succession], *Verzamelde Opstellen* vol. 2, 77-105. Utrecht/Antwerp: Uitgeverij Het Spectrum, 1978.

Groen van Prinsterer, Guillaume. *Ter Nagedachtenis van Stahl*. Amsterdam: Höveker, 1862.

Kohn, Hans, ed. *German History: Some New German Views*. London: George Allen & Unwin, 1954.

Meyer, R.W. *Leibniz and the Seventeenth-Century Revolution*, trans. J.P. Stern. Cambridge, England: Bowes and Bowes, 1952.

Nicolson, Harold. *The Congress of Vienna: A Study in Allied Unity, 1812-1822*. London: Constable, 1946.

Savigny, Friedrich Carl von. *Of the Vocation of Our Age for Legislation and Jurisprudence*, trans. Abraham Hayward. Union, NJ: Lawbook Exchange, 2002.

Schnabel, Franz. "The Bismarck Problem." In *German History: Some New German Views*, ed. Hans Kohn, 65-93. London: George Allen & Unwin, 1954.

Schoeps, Hans-Joachim. *Bismarck über Zeitgenossen, Zeitgenossen über Bismarck*. Frankfurt am Main/Berlin/Vienna: Ullstein Sachbuch, 1972.

Sheehan, James J. *German History 1770-1866*. Oxford: Clarendon Press, 1989.

Taylor, A. J. P. *Bismarck: The Man and the Statesman*. New York: Knopf, 1955.

Tocqueville, Alexis de. *The Old Regime and the French Revolution*, trans. Stuart Gilbert. Garden City, NY: Doubleday,

1955.

Wallmann, Johannes. *Kirchengeschichte Deutschlands seit der Reformation*. 5th revised and expanded ed. Tübingen: Mohr Siebeck, 2000.

Wines, Roger. "The Imperial Circles, Princely Diplomacy, and Imperial Reform, 1681–1714." *Journal of Modern History* 39, no. 1 (1967): 1–29.

Index